Chesuncook

Donald R. Goulet and
Frederick J. Moore III

AuthorHouse™
1663 Liberty Drive, Suite 200
Bloomington, IN 47403
www.authorhouse.com
Phone: 1-800-839-8640

© 2008 Donald R. Goulet and Frederick J. Moore III. All rights reserved.

No part of this book may be reproduced, stored in a retrieval system, or transmitted by any means without the written permission of the author.

First published by AuthorHouse   7/16/2008

ISBN: 978-1-4343-9400-2 (e)
ISBN: 978-1-4343-9398-2 (sc)
ISBN: 978-1-4343-9399-9 (hc)

Printed in the United States of America
Bloomington, Indiana

This book is printed on acid-free paper.

Cover Design by Corey Laflamme

To Donna, my spouse, and my children, Karen, Keith and Kristen, who committed themselves to moving without complaint while I served our country throughout the northeastern United States and Canada.

WHY I WROTE THIS BOOK

Before I started writing this book, I identified seven goals. One stands out as being of the greatest importance -- to promote the Greater Glory of God. The other six, in no particular order:

- Obtain recognition for Frederick Moore III as a protector of his Passamaquoddy people and explain his contribution to law enforcement and national jurisprudence.

- Examine psychological issues as they pertain to mental illness in hopes of helping others.

- Celebrate Father Capodanno's heroic Vietnam sacrifice in the name of Christ to the world.

- Foster a better understanding of the northeastern tribes of Native Americans, their culture and struggle for survival and power.

- Guide other law enforcement officers who face conditions similar to what I encountered in 1997 and 1998.

- Generate a modest income for myself, Fred and others involved in telling this story.

ACKNOWLEDGEMENTS

St. John was Christ's youngest apostle. He died a natural death in the year 100. He lived for the Greater Glory of God.

I profoundly thank my wife and three children for bearing with me and supporting me for the last two years while I wrote this book.

Without the computer and typing experience of Shirley Wells, former FBI secretary and stenographer, this book would have not been possible. Thanks Shirl.

I thank editor Dave Griffiths for his superior work in revising this work and asking me the questions that needed to be asked.

To author Mark LaFlamme, thanks for your words and acts of encouragement and support. I owe you big time. To Corey, Mark's wife, thanks for the exceptional book cover.

I further wish to acknowledge all of the men and women in law enforcement and the armed forces who I have known over the years for being who you are and doing what you do. I especially wish to thank management, the agents and support personnel in the Boston office of the FBI for not giving up on me when the road got rough in 1997 and 1998.

I would like to recognize the Slaves of the Immaculate Heart of Mary, a Rhode Island-based community of Catholic nuns who provided insight into the references I made to numerous apostles in this book. I gained a lot of insight from their book, "Book of Saints to Remember," which was published in the 1960s.

I further wish to thank all of the doctors and nurses who have helped me through the recovery process after my downfall.

TABLE OF CONTENTS

Chapter 1	Beginning a Life in "Little Canada"	15
Chapter 2	Becoming a United States Marine	21
Chapter 3	From the Halls of Montezuma	29
Chapter 4	Back to Real Life	61
Chapter 5	Street Agent	73
Chapter 6	Early Life on the Passamaquoddy Indian Reservation and Brief History and Culture	95
Chapter 7	Going Operational	107
Chapter 8	The Trial (January 28, 1994)	139
Chapter 9	Conflicts in the Courts (The Boots, Trapilo and Pasquantino Cases)	145
Chapter 10	The Manifestations of Mental Disorders	149
Chapter 11	Fall into perdition and a glimpse of Heaven	167
Chapter 12	The Road to Recovery and Return to Work	173
Chapter 13	2002 - 2008	183

INTRODUCTION

St. Peter the Apostle of Christ, the first Pope of the Catholic Church. He carries the keys to the kingdom. He was crucified upside down at his own request on June 29, A.D. 67. He died for the Greater Glory of God.

It was the first week of March 1998 at the Massachusetts General Hospital, 6th- floor Psychiatric Unit. The stocky, dark-haired man clad in dark blue pajamas paced back and forth. He stopped in front of my door and displayed his many and varied karate-like moves. He looked Hispanic, and in my warped thinking, I assumed he was my "personal protector." What a brilliant move by the FBI! They had set me up in a psychiatric unit. No one would ever think of looking for me there. More importantly, my family was safe and sound. I had been assured of that.

For the next several days, I continued to suffer delusions of grandeur and persecution, misidentification, paranoia, depression, excessive unfounded guilt, mania and scrupulousness -- all common maladies of the psychotic.

My wife Donna was there daily, supporting me, telling the doctors that I wasn't getting better, insisting that my medication be changed.

Finally, they tried the drug Trilafon, 32 milligrams worth. Within 48 hours, my condition improved dramatically. The psychosis, delusions, paranoia, depression, guilt and scrupulousness were in remission.

My wife brought a cassette that featured the soft rhythm of waves lapping the shoreline. It was called "Oceans." One piece in particular, my favorite, had a background of gently pounding drums reminding me of the Passamaquoddy people and the great state of Maine I had so recently served. Coupled with the Trilafon, the music transported me to a world of peace and tranquility.

A war fought long ago but still ever present, job-related stress, PTSD triggers and alcohol dependency had brought me to my knees. I fought it, but mental illness prevailed. Later on, my FBI street agent colleagues told me it was God's will, that He knew I had had enough and that what happened was for the best.

My faith was sorely tested back in 1998. I had been an on-again/off-again Catholic for 32 years. My illness eventually brought me to the edge of perdition and ultimately to a deeper understanding of Catholicism and a renewed devotion to Christ our Redeemer.

Fred Moore was born in the spring of 1960 on the Pleasant Point Indian Reservation. He was one of the People of the Dawn, a description of all Northeastern tribes whose land is bathed by the early morning sun. The Passamaquoddies are the easternmost of all American tribes. Since the Pleasant Point Indian Reservation borders a bay, they are also referred to as "Sypayik," which means "the edge."

Fred is a blood member of a proud race that has inhabited the shores of Passamaquoddy Bay for 10,000 years. In his youth, he went through periods of rebellion, defiance and radicalism. With the help and wisdom of his elders, he changed his life, eventually becoming police chief of the Pleasant Point Reservation. He dedicated his life to protecting the sovereignty of his people and enforcing the law. At one highly dangerous juncture, he subjected himself to "dishonor." As we shall see, Fred's decision to go undercover to defeat a smuggling operation by some nasty Native Americans from another tribe led to suspicions among his own people that he was a crook.

I got to know Fred in 1992 when he worked undercover for the FBI and the Royal Canadian Mounted Police. The result of a two-year investigation, including trial and sentencing (and seven months of undercover work), was that the U.S. Supreme Court upheld the "Fraud By Wire" statute as it applies to smuggling. Where once it was impossible to get a conviction naming a foreign government as a victim, it is now commonplace and worldwide in application, thanks in part to that case.

Fred also protected the sovereignty of the Passamaquoddy Tribe and was directly responsible for the conviction of notorious criminals such as Mohawk Warrior Society "War Chief" Francis Boots from the Akwesasne Indian Reservation -- which crosses the international border from Ontario and Quebec to St. Regis, New York -- and Stanley Johnson from Nova Scotia. The two operated a major illegal tobacco distribution network throughout the Canadian Maritime Provinces that harmed parts of the Canadian economy. It started with large tractor-trailer loads of tobacco shipped from the southeastern U.S. to the Akwesasne Reservation, where it was purchased at a very low price.

Estimates were that smuggling enterprises, mostly controlled by the Mohawk Warrior Society, deprived the Canadian government of some $1 billion a year in lost tax revenue. That in turn affected the Canadian single-payer health care system, which gets most of its revenues from "sin taxes." And more than half the legitimate tobacco distribution enterprises in parts of Canada had to shut down because they couldn't compete with the Warriors.

In the late 1990s, the Canadian attorney general filed a massive lawsuit in the United States seeking to retrieve damages from large tobacco companies involved in the illegal tobacco trade (Attorney General of Canada vs. R. J. Reynolds Tobacco Holdings Inc., or Canada vs. United States, District Court for the Northern District of New York). The civil lawsuit was thrown out of federal court on the grounds that it violated a rule prohibiting a foreign government from collecting lost revenues using the United States as its collection agency.

Also convicted in the Boots criminal case was a high-level Canadian public official from Nova Scotia whom Johnson bribed to protect the enterprise. Despite frenzied attempts by individuals inside and outside of the tribe to discredit Fred and the investigation, Fred and the FBI prevailed. Once the results of the case were known, Fred was overwhelmingly elected twice to serve as the tribe's representative to the Maine Legislature.

Was it chance, circumstance or pre-destination that led a highly motivated and experienced FBI street agent assigned to the Bangor Maine Resident Office, meaning me, to link up with Police Chief Fred Moore? This book will answer that question.

The story didn't end with the Boots case. From there, working with Senior Special Agent Charles "Chuck" Gifford from the office of the Department of Interior's Inspector General's office, we investigated several Native American allegations of wrongdoing concerning Interior and Bureau of Indian Affairs (BIA) programs, and including indirect and direct loans to Passamaquoddy Technology, a company involved in research and development of large-scale environmental scrubbing of huge smokestacks.

Over five years we worked together closely, occasionally sharing fruits of the sea such as steamer clams and lobsters. Those BIA investigations are quite sensitive, and they have led so far to one conviction. Chuck Gifford and I investigated well-known Bangor property manager Darrell Cooper for stealing Native American funds from the Maliseet Gardens Property owned by the Maliseet tribe. Cooper pleaded guilty to converting to his own use more than $300,000 owed the Maliseets, which he received from rent collections.

Also, the Passamaquoddy people owe the Bureau of Indian Affairs $3 million or $4 million from direct and indirect loans that Passamaquoddy Technology obtained from BIA through the tribe.

Back to the Mohawks: As I debriefed Fred, known as "Moose" on the reservation, and began to appreciate the scope of the criminal enterprise, I had an inspiration that encompassed my intense experiences as a Marine in Vietnam. I would dedicate my Native American work to Father Vincent Capodanno, a Catholic chaplain who was killed in Vietnam on Sept. 4, 1967. "Father Cap" was with Mike Company, 3rd Battalion, 5th Marines (the Fighting Fifth), my outfit, when we were ambushed by some 500 North Vietnamese Army troops. He died while tending to his fallen Marines, giving some the Last Rites and treating others for their wounds. For that, he was awarded the Congressional Medal of Honor.

I also dedicated the Native American work to Cpl. Vernon "Randy" Randolph, who was killed on Feb. 7, 1968, five months after I left 'Nam. We'd been corresponding regularly right up to the time of his death. Randy was my best friend in Vietnam and was part Native American from the Iroquois nation.

I had been spared what I thought was certain death in at least 12 encounters with the enemy. While being evacuated by helicopter during Operation Swift the day after Father Cap died, I bowed my head, said a prayer of thanks to our Lord and promised to dedicate my life to the betterment of humankind.

In April 1992, the contact I'd been waiting for finally materialized in Bangor. Police Chief Fred Moore was on the line to the FBI office. I'd brought the U.S. Customs Service, the Bureau of Indian Affairs and the Inspector General's Office at Interior into the picture. Chief Moore told me he'd been approached by some Mohawk Indians from the Akwesasne Indian Reservation in upstate New York.

The Mohawks wanted to partner with Moore and Anthony Stanley, another Passamaquoddy tribal member, to smuggle tobacco into Canada from the Pleasant Point Indian Reservation in Perry, Maine. Chief Moore wanted the FBI's guidance. Our immediate reaction was that if the Mohawks traveled from New York to Maine to do a smuggling deal that included bribery of a law enforcement officer (Fred Moore), then the Racketeering Influenced Corrupt Organization (RICO) statute would probably apply.

And in this case, bribery fell under the Interstate Travel In Aid To Racketeering (ITAR) Act, a derivative of RICO. The attempted bribe was $20 per case of smuggled tobacco, and Fred would deliver 50 to 60 cases per four-hour trip across Passamaquoddy Bay to New Brunswick, Canada, and back (although the first one took 10 hours, thanks to tough sea conditions, fog, rain and wind). Moore's plan was that he would give Anthony Stanley, also known as "Pluto," his share and turn over his own share to the FBI. (A cautionary note: There are two Stanleys involved here. One is Anthony Stanley from the Pleasant Point Indian Reservation, and the other was Stanley Johnson, known as "Fat Man," from the Mic Mac tribe of Indians in Truro, Nova Scotia.)

Fred, who had had no contact with Boots or the Mohawk Warrior Society for 15 years or so, had been approached by Anthony Stanley to smuggle tobacco across the bay to St. Andrews, New Brunswick. Francis Boots, through a woman named Beverly Pierro, had approached Stanley because he and Moore had attended a sit-in at the Akewasasne reservation in about 1977. One reason he targeted Fred is that the police chief was known as a good boat navigator. But Boots never realized how seriously Fred had taken his police oath of office.

I arranged to meet with Fred the next morning. Before Moore's phone call, having been told about the case by the Bureau of Indian Affairs and the Customs Service, I had called Sgt. Ralph Bridges of the Calais (Maine) Police Department to assess Moore's character. He vouched for him, calling Moore "a pretty damn good guy." I also spoke with Assistant U.S. Attorney Jim McCarthy in his Bangor office. He seconded Bridges' sentiments.

So Fred's return phone call to me turned out to be a life-changing event for many of us. Many would be convicted. Many more would scatter. Many would get nervous and some would try to thwart our efforts. National and international jurisprudence would be changed forever. The FBI would join forces with the Royal Canadian Mounted Police in a two-year operation that would generate mutual respect and admiration. The honor and glory of both agencies would be enhanced. The Inspector General's Office at Interior would assign its most experienced agent on the East Coast to help us out. And the Bangor FBI office would look into many collateral issues springing from Fred's work against the Mohawks who arrived on his reservation for the purpose of smuggling.

That's hardly what I expected in quiet little Bangor, where I'd been transferred from New York City, at my request. I hoped to finish my career in a relaxed atmosphere, investigating a bank robbery here or there, handling other investigations in a leisurely fashion, then moseying off to enjoy the rest of my life with my wife and children. Piece of cake, I figured.

The day after that phone call, I met Fred at our office. He arrived about 10 a.m. in a large silver GMC pickup, with his wife Rachel and two young daughters, Kristine, 4, and Kathleen, 2. (After our meeting, he took them all shopping in Bangor as he made this a special family trip.) Rachel was seven months pregnant. We shook hands and he handed me a large white plastic bag holding 16 plastic containers.

Each one contained 200 grams of loose tobacco, the preferred form for smuggling. In fact, rolling your own tobacco was a big business in the Maritime Provinces of Canada. There was more profit in "roll your own," and it was much harder to trace than cigarette packs, which are supposed to have revenue stamps affixed to them.

Two Mohawks named Dewey Lazore and Ellwyn Cook had given them to him. Each container was eggshell white and had a blue dot in the center of its twist-off lid. That transfer of containers would establish the groundwork for enforcing the ITAR statute. The U.S. attorney would introduce those containers as evidence of the first bribery attempt of Chief Moore when the matter came to trial.

Fred had obtained the tobacco from the Mohawks the day before. The next day, before I talked to Fred for the first time, he had spoken with Bureau of Indian Affairs investigator William Lorentino. Lorentino, having heard about the Mohawks' approach to Fred, asked Fred to meet with the Mohawks to see what they wanted. What brought the FBI into the case was that Cook and Lazore had driven across state lines to meet with the Passamaquoddy police chief at Pleasant Point.

I asked Fred to come into the office again. That's when Fred told us about Francis Boots, who headed the smuggling operation. The plan was for Fred and Pluto to smuggle the tobacco from the Pleasant Point

Indian Reservation across Passamaquoddy Bay. At the time, we didn't know who was to receive the tobacco. In return, Fred and Pluto would split $20 per case of tobacco smuggled into St. Andrews. (A case of tobacco weighs about 6,000 grams or 14.3 pounds. So a smuggle of 50 cases would amount to a little over 700 pounds.)

The Mohawks talked about bringing in tractor-trailer loads and establishing a major illegal business at Pleasant Point. The 16 plastic containers were gifts to Fred and Pluto, to be sold if they wished. And as I recall, the loose tobacco originated in the southern states.

While debriefing Moore, I sized him up. He was physically fit, appeared to be quite strong, and was mentally sharp. He stood about 5'8', weighed around 175 pounds, and was wearing a brown leather jacket and dark gray pants. His complexion was reddish and he had a crew cut -- definitely Native American in appearance, I figured. Yes, he'd make a great witness. I'm sure that Moore was sizing me up at the same time.

After Moore left, I called my supervisor, Supervisory Special Agent (SSA) Jim Powers in the Boston FBI office. I briefed him on the Mohawk plan and asked him to run name checks.

I also examined federal statues that could be brought to bear. I reasoned that if a criminal organization was based in the United States and smuggled goods into a foreign country to avoid paying various taxes and duties, then Title 18, United States Code, Section 1343, Fraud by Wire, might apply. That applies to crimes of fraud perpetuated by interstate communication lines, such as a telephone, computer or fax machine. Also relevant were the Interstate Transportation in Aid to Racketeering (ITAR) and bribery statutes.

About two hours later, Powers called back to say that the name Francis Boots set off "bells and whistles in FBI headquarters." Boots had been of interest because he was the war chief during the Mohawk uprising along the New York-Canada border in 1990. The Mohawk Warriors took a pro-gambling position against the traditional Mohawks, who at the time were anti-gambling. The ensuing result was a major firefight, which broke out between the two warring parties.

At the time, the Mohawk Warrior Society also opposed the sale of land owned by the Oka Indian Reservation in Oka, Quebec, to the Canadian government, which turned into a major firefight between the Mohawks and the Surete du Quebec provincial police. In that encounter, Corporal Marcel LeMay of the Surete du Quebec was shot and killed. No one seems to know what Boots did at the uprising, except for the fact that as war chief, he allegedly controlled the activities of the warriors engaged.

If it could have been proven that he directed the warriors' fire, he would have gone to jail. Like New York crime boss John Gotti (who died in jail), he covered his rear end carefully -- that is, until he got involved with Fred. He was of interest to various law enforcement sources for many years. I told Powers I would open a "corruption of a local public official" matter, coupled with the Fraud By Wire statute.

I also contacted the Royal Canadian Mounted Police in New Brunswick, Canada. Boots, as Warrior Society war chief, a self-declared position that gave him great power over his people, led some 250 warriors. So the RCMP definitely wanted to work with the FBI on this case.

Then I went to Assistant U.S. Attorney Jim McCarthy, who called my notion about the Fraud By Wire statute "interesting." At the time, I didn't think that the law had been applied in this type of case before. The next day, I sent a teletype, which included my feelings about the potential for a joint operation with the Canadians, to FBI headquarters in Washington and the Bureau's Albany (New York) Division. What I told them was that a major smuggling route was about to be opened between St. Andrews, New Brunswick, and the Pleasant Point Indian Reservation.

As luck would have it, that same day a Bureau official told me that when my teletype crossed the desk of Director William Sessions, he was discussing the issue of lost revenue to Canada due to smuggling with his counterpart, the commissioner of the RCMP. From then on, Sessions had one of his assistant directors check in on our operations almost daily.

That afternoon, I drove to the reservation. Fred and I met in a remote location and for the next day and a half we discussed the case in great detail. I asked Fred why Pluto had approached him. In the late 1970s, he and Pluto had been involved in a sit-in at the Akwesasne Indian Reservation in New York, where they met Francis Boots.

We also knew that Fred himself had had a few scrapes with the law. He was convicted of felonious assault and unrelated charges of night hunting and illegal clam digging. Fred had gotten into a fight in the late 1970s and broke his opponent's arm, which landed him in prison for less than a year. In the mid-1980s, he applied for and got a pardon from Maine Governor William Brennan. That happened before the tribal governor appointed him police chief.

While at the sit-in, he met with the Mohawk tribal elders, who told him what was going on behind the scenes. They said the warriors were involved in gun running, cocaine distribution and other smuggling ventures, and warned that the warriors were not what they claimed to be. Hearing that, Fred left the sit-in and returned home. His explanation of his own past and brief flirtation with Mohawk protesters left me with the clear impression that we could investigate and prosecute the smuggling matter.

During our remote meeting, Chief Moore explained the cultural differences between the Mohawk and Passamaquoddy tribes. Some

300 years earlier, Mohawk warriors invaded what is now Maine with the intent of establishing control over all the tribes. But after they attacked the Penobscots, the Passamaquoddy tribe joined forces with their neighbors and beat back the Mohawks.

Back to the here and now, Moore said the Mohawks not only wanted to establish a new and safe smuggling route, free from law enforcement interference. They also wanted a permanent presence on the Pleasant Point Indian Reservation. Maine got their attention because their violent activities along the New York border with Canada in 1990 had pretty much closed down that smuggling avenue. Some of the Mohawk Warriors and their associates had been running guns and cocaine into Canada as well as loose and packaged tobacco.

Years earlier, Boots told Fred that he was interested in the Passamaquoddy territory. Now Fred was certain that allowing Mohawks on his reservation would lead to drug and arms smuggling and threaten the sovereignty of the Passamaquoddy people. At that point, it dawned on me that this was much more than mere tobacco smuggling.

Our conversation touched me deeply. So I brought up a few personal matters, including the heroic sacrifices of Father Vincent Capodanno and Vernon Randolph, who was part Native American. I told him that I was dedicating my work on the smuggling operation to the remembrance of these two men. So here I found fulfillment of the promise I had made long ago as I was airlifted from that battlefield in Southeast Asia.

I returned home that evening, speculating that the case would be resolved in 60 to 90 days. I held Chief Moore in high regard. Not only did he come forward to reveal this attempt on his integrity, but he also committed to recording conversations with the bad guys during the investigation -- the best evidence available.

I also thought about the fishing trip my family and I were planning for the end of May and concluded that I would have to forego it until the following year. The previous spring, we had fished on Lake Chesuncook in northwestern Maine. It boasted a large population of landlocked salmon in the two- to five-pound range and was a joy to fish. My family would miss it dearly this year, but duty called. The name Chesuncook is an American Indian name meaning Big Water. I had a couple Buds and retired for the evening.

CHAPTER 1

Beginning a Life in "Little Canada"

St. Thomas, also known as Didimus, was Christ's apostle who doubted his resurrection, until he, Thomas, placed his fingers in the wounds of Christ. He was martyred by being stabbed to death in the year 0074. He died for the Greater Glory of God.

Lewiston, Maine, was a thriving mill town from the late 1800s to the early 1980s. It boasted several wool mills and shoe shops, as well as a bleachery that manufactured white sheets under the brand name of Lady Pepperill. At one point, Bates Mill employed up to 5,000 workers. The factories in Lewiston and Auburn, its sister city across the Androscoggin River, drew thousands of French Canadian families from Quebec. By far, most of them were Catholic and they made up about 60 percent of the Lewiston population.

In the early 1920s, my father, Antonio "Tony" Goulet, immigrated to Lewiston from a farm in Disraeli, Quebec, with his father, mother, six brothers and four sisters. My mother, Cecile Galarneau, was born a French Canadian Catholic in Auburn. Her family had immigrated from Canada a couple generations earlier.

Lewiston's premier landmark is the enormous Basilica of St. Peter and St. Paul. The inner city is composed mostly of four- to five-story tenement houses where most of the French Catholic immigrants lived in walk-up apartments. Adjacent to the northern bank of the Androscoggin River is a neighborhood that came to be known as "Little Canada," my home.

With the help of a nurse, my cousin Theresa Goulet, I entered the world in a five-room apartment on Lincoln Street on Oct. 8, 1947 -- a sunny, blue-skied, cool Saturday. They named me Donald Raymond Joseph Goulet.

My father was a finish carpenter by trade and worked for Goulet Construction, owned by my uncles Ernest and Wilfred Goulet. In the mid- to late-'50s, it closed and he went to work for Clark Shoe in Auburn as a carpenter and maintenance worker. My mother Cecile was a shoe shop worker. Her job was to apply glue to shoe bottoms for the soles. I had two older sisters, Monique and Venise, and three years after I appeared, Bertrand (Ti-Bert) was born.

We were a very poor family. I got two pairs of shoes a year, and the soles were detached on half of them. On Fridays we ate bananas and two-day-old bread; that's what my parents could afford. But we always had a big Sunday dinner after Mass, either chicken or pot roast. We also ate spaghetti and meatballs on occasion. For breakfast, we usually had crepes, which were cheap to prepare with milk, flour, eggs and salt. We also ate a lot of salt pork. Poor, yes, but a happy family.

And just like so many people in Lewiston and Auburn, we were bilingual, speaking French at home and English at school. That may sound like quite a hassle, but to us it was perfectly natural.

During my early years, I was heavily influenced by television series such as "Sergeant Preston of the Yukon," "Davy Crockett," "Rough Riders," "Gunsmoke," "The Rifleman," "Sky King" and "Rin Tin Tin."

Ti-Bert's favorite was "Howdy Doody." The popular songs of that time were "The Three Bells" by Jim Ed Brown and his sisters Maxine and Brownie, and "Indian Love Call" by Nelson Eddy and Jeannette McDonald. "Lassie Come Home" was a prominent movie when Ti-Bert was born.

We were a deeply religious Catholic family. Attendance at mass on Sunday was mandatory and when we were older, participating in the sacraments was routine. We strictly followed the Ten Commandments and our parents, priests, nuns and brothers taught us to love Christ, as He was the answer to everlasting life and to peace on earth. In the early days, we did not eat meat on Fridays and we went to Confession almost weekly, although I doubted that any of us at that age really needed to go so frequently.

I loved my kid brother Ti-Bert (he was a small kid) so much so that I picked on him relentlessly, in part, I suppose, to develop his character. In turn, he attacked me with and without provocation. We were close.

After a long day of hard work, my father's habit was to go to the local bar at 4:30 or 5 p.m. I don't remember its name, but I do recall that it was in among the tenements on Walnut Street, and someone named Camille Ouellette owned it. My father had a couple beers, came home and had supper. As I reached seven or eight years old, I began going with him and joined the social scene. The patrons were always buying me potato chips and snacks and glasses of Coca-Cola. In turn, I followed my father's example and sprinkled salt in my Coke as he sprinkled salt in his beer.

Once a week Dad and Mom went to the local "social club" for a few drinks. That was an important part of their culture and I never begrudged them that time because they worked so hard every day.

On one occasion, when I was about nine, my mother and father took me along to a social club on Walnut Street to show me off. One day, I had a salted Coke and then went to the restroom, where I found a $20 bill on the floor. I turned the money over to Dad and he asked if anyone in the club was short 20 bucks. No one claimed it, so the next day he turned it in to the police station in the event that someone lost it.

No one did, and after a few weeks the police gave him the money, which he spent on a BB gun and BBs for me. He told me to share it with Ti-Bert. Big mistake. Even though I had surpassed six years old, the age of reason (knowing the difference between right and wrong, as defined by the Catholic Church), Ti-Bert had not.

In the basement, Dad had built us a fort made of plywood. It boasted parapets, fighting positions to put our army men on, etc. Bert and I spent hours shooting at our "enemies." Behind the fort was a series of shelves that Dad stocked with snowshoe hare meat (rabbit hunting was his great passion) covered with gravy and canned in glass Ball jars.

One day, while Ti-Bert was shooting it out with the enemy, a sharp "ping" reverberated through the basement. He had hit one of the glass jars. The contents began to spill out, and that must have intrigued my little brother because he proceeded to fire into the attacking masses of glass Ball jars coming right at him. Re-slaughtering all the rabbits, he nailed every jar, some 35 to 40 of them. Gravy and liquids leaked everywhere.

Then guilt set in. Ti-Bert rushed upstairs and told me what he had done. I looked at him and he started blubbering. I knew then and there that he had reached that magical age of reason whose fundamental precept is the discernment between right and wrong, good and evil.

Scared at how we imagined Dad might react, we kept our mouths shut. A couple days went by and Dad went downstairs for a jar of snowshoe hare in gravy. Within a minute or two, he came back up, looked at us, and asked, "Where's the gun?" He kept it from us for six months. Not another word was spoken. We weren't yelled at, screamed at, told that he was disappointed in our behavior or anything like that. He simply deprived us of the BB gun.

I attended first grade at St. Mary's grammar school in Little Canada. When I turned seven, we moved from Lincoln Street to Blake Street and I switched to St. Peter and Paul, where I graduated in 1961. I then entered St. Dominic High School, graduating in 1965.

I had a core of friends in those days, all French Canadian -- Normand Saucier, Roger Perreault, Donnie Boutin, Ray LeBlond, Dick and Ray Robert, Reynaldo Janelle, Lucien Michael, Norm Caron, Bob Roy, Pete Gagnon, Mike Tremblay, Paul Bizier, Bobby Drouin, Dick Malo, Bob Begin, Paul Ouellette and George Roy. Their collective characters -- devotion to Catholicism, love of sports, love of their parents -- helped shape my own values.

In grammar school and high school, we learned from Dominican nuns and the Brothers of the Sacred Heart. In those days, the high school was segregated into male and female components. I think the philosophy was that less contact with the opposite sex meant fewer distractions and a better learning environment.

The nuns and brothers were great teachers. They were experts in education, had no outside distractions and treated us with respect. Once in a while, if someone was out of line, a few of the brothers imposed a minor physical punishment on the perpetrator, twisting an ear or bouncing a piece of chalk off a noggin, or whizzing a chalk board eraser past a head. They were small corrections, but very effective in maintaining discipline.

Meanwhile, I did my share financially. Delivering newspapers for the Lewiston Sun Journal, my route covered Walnut, Ash, Pierce and Bartlett streets. I was out on the streets at 4 a.m. seven days a week and

I finished at 5:30 a.m. after delivering about 120 newspapers. With tips, I earned $6 to $8 a week

In 1957, I joined Boy Scout Troop 118. At the age of 13, I was an Eagle Scout (the youngest in Maine at the time, as I recall), senior patrol leader and member of the Order of the Arrow. I also won the Ad Altarei Dei award, which recognized a Scout's devotion to the Catholic Church -- in my case, serving mass as an altar boy at St. Peter and Paul's Church from 1954 until 1960.

In 1959, I led a Scout patrol on a hike from downtown Lewiston to Sabattus Mountain, which is next to Sabattus Lake about five miles northeast of town. It became a special place for me, as a year later I hiked it by myself. On that day, I stood at the edge of a cliff, took in the trees and woods of central Maine below me, and prayed to our Lord, asking him to guide me in life.

I was approaching the age of financial responsibility and I wanted to provide the best I could for the family I hoped to have some day. While praying on that mountain, something told me I would suffer greatly in my life, and that would be the price to pay for working myself out of poverty. At that moment, that little cliff on Sabattus Mountain became one of my most cherished spots.

A few years later, in 1965, I brought my girlfriend to the mountain to share its beauty. (I'll keep her name and background to myself, as I don't want any hurt feelings.) A few months later I proposed to her and we became engaged.

CHAPTER 2

BECOMING A UNITED STATES MARINE

St. Matthew was a tax collector and became one of Christ's apostles. He was martyred while saying mass in the year A.D. 65. He died for the Greater Glory of God.

On a nice day back in June 1961, I remember walking around the neighborhoods near downtown Lewiston with two friends -- Dick Robert and his cousin Ray Robert. Like teenage boys anywhere, we poked at each as we walked. As happens when kids have time on their hands and energy to burn, things escalated. At one point, Dick and Ray spotted an empty trashcan lying on the side of the street. And that gave them an idea.

Grabbing my arms and legs (I was 5' 3" and all of 110 pounds), they stuffed me in the trashcan, butt first, feet and hands sticking straight upward, then walked away laughing. I found myself in an acutely embarrassing pickle. No matter how I squirmed, I couldn't free myself. Fortunately, an older man coming out of Coulombe's Market at the intersection of Blake and Birch Street helped extricate me from the barrel.

I wasn't really angry with Ray or Dick; it was all good fun between boys. But I was a bit upset with myself. I hadn't given the two of them enough of a fight. Right then and there, I swore to be a tougher fighter. I would become a United States Marine. (By the way, four years later, Dick and Ray were stars on the St. Dominic's High School ice hockey team that won the New England championship.)

First came my education, or so I thought. After graduating from St. Dom's in 1965, I enrolled at the University of Maine in Orono with the intention of studying forestry. But two events turned me toward the Corps. During a dormitory bull session two or three months into my freshman year, a television news broadcast silenced all of us. Several Marines had been killed and wounded during a fierce firefight in Vietnam. We saw photos of the dead and wounded.

Immediately I felt that I no longer belonged to the fraternity of academics. By the lights of my conscience, I could not stay in school while Americans my age were waging war. I told myself, "I have to join these guys and do my part for my country." In all honesty, my grades weren't that great, I was poor, and I began to think that joining the Corps would be a way to improve my life.

My attitudes solidified as winter approached. In December, I attended a St. Dom's hockey game without my girlfriend. When they played the National Anthem, I got emotional and felt a deep sense of devotion and loyalty to our great nation. Slightly misty-eyed, I decided to enlist in the Marine Corps, ask to be a rifleman, and volunteer for combat duty in Vietnam.

In return, I'd get room and board, three square meals a day, $85 a month, and a chance to use the G.I. Bill later to further my education. That way, I'd fulfill my father's dream that I get a college degree. Then I'd look for work in law enforcement or wildlife management.

On Feb. 28, 1966, I joined the Marine Corps. I took the oath to defend and protect the country and headed to boot camp in Parris Island, South Carolina. They put me in Platoon 146 with 79 other "boots." There, I met a special friend, Jim Hamfeldt from Morristown, N.J. There were also two other "pukes" from Maine, David Poirier and Roy Woodside, both from the Portland area.

Woodside was a tall, gaunt, 17-year-old redheaded kid who the drill instructors selected for "special treatment." Being slightly uncoordinated, his missteps led to physical fitness punishment for the rest of us on numerous occasions. Each time he messed up, the platoon paid.

For example, when Roy turned right instead of left on command, it became our problem. The DIs pushed him around and occasionally struck him and gave us all 100 push-ups to make amends for his errors. Roy's age, gangly physique and mild lack of coordination appeared to make him a weak link, and the DIs were all over him. But it turned out that he was tougher than most.

The drill instructors did their best to break Woodside, but without success. The kid had guts. Eventually, Woodside and Poirier were badly wounded in Vietnam. Dave lost his right leg beneath the knee and Roy took a machine gun burst in the left arm, side and leg.

Boot camp was brutal for all of us, no matter how physically fit we were coming in. Each one of us eventually got a punch to the stomach or head to get our attention. We ran about six miles a day and, on one occasion, I recall going without any sleep for some 36 hours.

I also remember seeing a Marine fall from a 30-foot rope climb and land on his pack and rifle. He lay there motionless. The fall had broken his M-14 rifle in two. The DIs ran to his side, picked up the broken butt of the rifle and screamed, "He broke my Marine Corps rifle!" repeatedly.

But we all knew the Marine had probably broken his back. (We never found out if he had broken his back, or if he remained in the Corps). They removed us from the area and an ambulance arrived. Then they marched us back to the squad bay where a drill instructor lined us up at attention and walked up and down and asked each one of us, "Will you ever break my Marine Corps rifle?"

"No sir!" we said, one after the other.

At each response, the DI jammed the broken rifle butt into the stomach. Actually, it was funny to the guys who were struck early as they watched the expressions of the other "turds" flinching just before they got jammed in the guts.

It wasn't all pain. And even the humiliation could have a humorous side to it. Take the case of Danny Nicklow, who'd been selected by the drill instructors to escort, feed, water and exercise an imaginary dog known as "Blood and Guts." One morning after breakfast, we were all standing in formation when the DIs approached Danny and asked how the dog was doing.

Danny had his right hand up in a perpendicular position holding an imaginary leash to an imaginary dog. He told them that Blood and Guts had consumed three dozen eggs, four pounds of bacon, eight slices of toast and half a gallon of coffee. In that case, the DIs asked, had he given the dog a chance to relieve himself?

No he hadn't. So the DIs ordered Danny to fall out of formation with Blood and Guts and take him for a walk in the nearby fields. I'll never forget the sight of Danny Nicklow "walking" that dog. After Blood and Guts did his business, Danny returned to the platoon and reported that the dog was ready for the day.

Along the way, pride began to enter the picture. For instance, mastering the group skill of marching to cadence was a relief of sorts compared to much of the boot camp brutality. When we marched, the

DIs left us alone physically for the most part and they "sang" to us in a soothing melodious cadence.

And there was room for some humor, although it was humor of a particularly savage Marine Corps variety.

One time a DI walked up to a recruit and showed him a picture of his wife.

He asked, "Do you like my wife, Private?"

"Yes sir."

"Do you know that liking leads to loving and loving leads to making love [or words to that effect]? Do you want to love my wife, Private?"

Confused, the private said, "No sir."

Instantly, the DI punched the poor recruit in the belly, doubling him over. "Oh, she's not good enough for you, huh?"

Then he moved to the next recruit in line and asked the same questions. Asked if he'd like to make love to the DI's wife, the recruit said he would. Again, a hard punch to the belly. "Oh, you're a marriage breaker, huh?" or words to that effect. Damned if you do, damned if you don't.

After eight weeks of boot camp, the platoon went to Camp Geiger in North Carolina to join the infantry training regiment, where we were drilled in combat techniques at the squad, platoon and company levels. We were also introduced to machine guns, grenades, grenade launchers, rocket launchers and the like.

Then, finally, we went on leave. It was the summer of 1966, the year after the first Marine combat contingent went ashore in Vietnam. Knowing I was headed that way, I took 15 days to go home, hung around Sabattus Lake and horsed around with a few friends.

My next assignment was Camp LeJeune, N.C., where we were assigned to companies. A boot camp buddy, Danny Nicklow, Jim Hamfeltd, a kid from Harmony, Maine named Mike Gourley and I were assigned to an 81-millimeter mortar outfit. All day long in the crushing heat, we humped cases of mortar rounds.

After one particularly grueling July day, Danny suggested that we go to the Enlisted Man's Club for a few beers. I had never drunk beer before. It was illegal to drink as a teenager in Maine, and I never had the desire anyway. But now I was 18, and I could drink, as it was no stronger than 3.2 percent alcohol. Turns out I liked it, cool and refreshing, and after the first glass, I felt pretty good.

An hour later, I had polished off a pitcher, nearly two quarts, on my own and the rest of them had knocked back a lot of beer themselves. We went to supper and returned to the barracks, where I fell into a deep and restful sleep.

But the next morning was a different story. My head was pounding with pain. I was flushed, hot and nauseated. That was the first and last time I drank beer at Camp LeJeune.

In early August, we assembled in the barracks and the platoon sergeant asked for volunteers to fight in Vietnam. I stepped forward, as did Jim Hamfeltd and Mike Gourley. Our orders were cut, and that weekend we went on leave back home and said goodbye to family, friends and my fiance -- a relatively painful experience for me. Mom and Dad had tears in their eyes as I left from the Portland, Maine airport. So did my fiance. They all knew I was committed to the Corps and to this country and understood that this was what I had to do. It was a difficult parting for all.

At the end of August, we reported to Camp Pendleton, San Diego, for jungle warfare training. Marches with full field packs and rifles were the order of the day. And they were always "forced" marches, in which you march at double the normal gait with full field pack and rifle, covering 20 to 25 miles a day. Chesty Puller, the legendary Marine Corps general of World War 2, was our hero, and a popular song of the time was "96 Tears," by the Mysterians in 1966.

In the middle of September 1966, they flew us to Okinawa, a final stop before 'Nam. Training was almost nonexistent and we had time on our hands. One evening, I joined a bunch of Marines for a trip to the local Enlisted Man's Club. I hadn't had any alcohol since July.

Hard whiskey, a first for me, was selling for ten cents per shot glass. I ordered one, drank it down, and felt a nice buzz. It was a bit harsh, but heck, I was keeping up the tradition of the Corps -- hard-fighting, hard-drinking leathernecks. I ordered two more shots, drank them down and returned to the barracks feeling pretty doggone good. Sure enough, another painful hangover awaited me the next morning. I didn't drink again until we were in Vietnam.

CHAPTER 3

From the Halls of Montezuma

MIKE COMPANY, THIRD BATALLION, FIFTH MARINES, THE FIGHTING FIFTH

Father Vincent Robert Capodanno, Chaplain, United States Navy, severely wounded twice, facing great personal danger, tended to his dead and wounded Marines. While physically protecting the wounded Navy Corpsman Armando Leal, he was gunned down and received the Congressional Medal of Honor posthumously. He died for the Greater Glory of God.

I arrived in Vietnam in October 1966 and was assigned to help guard Chu Lai Air Base south of DaNang on the seacoast, with Mike Company, Third Battalion, Fifth Marines.

My second evening there, I went out on my first patrol. It was a night patrol. We would be guarding the northern flank of the air base. It had rained profusely that day. Walking down a trail, we came to a small, slow-moving stream. I was "tail end Charlie," and at 5'6", crossing it was a major obstacle. I was up to my chin in water, holding my rifle over my head, walking on the tips of my toes. I barely got through, but I did.

The next day, a truck carrying troops arrived at company headquarters. Who should disembark but Roland Guerette, a classmate of mine from the 2nd-grade through the 8th-grade at St. Peters Grammar School in Lewiston. We recognized each other and shook hands, and he offered me a Pall Mall, which I reluctantly smoked. I had never smoked before. I didn't like it at first, but not much later, when we came under sniper fire, I lit one up and it calmed my nerves and relieved my anxiety. I've been smoking cigarettes ever since then.

Over the next two months, Roland and I were together as often as possible. He had been assigned to the First Platoon; I was with the Third. A platoon usually was comprised of 36 to 44 Marines.

About two weeks after I spotted Roland, Mike Company was deployed to Hill 69, the new battalion headquarters seven or eight miles north of Chu Lai. Daily, we patrolled the rice paddies and villages within a two-mile radius of headquarters. One landmark, Hill 71, was in our patrol zone and manned by a platoon of Marines.

Right about then, when we were bivouacked just outside Tam Ky, I got a letter from my fiancé. She had fallen in love with another man and our relationship was over. I was surprised and devastated. There had been absolutely no sign of a problem with our relationship. I kept thinking of the song "Blue on Blue" by Bobby Vinton.

I'll never forget the way my squad, all 12 of them, responded to my Dear John letter. The night I got it, the squad collected four cans of Budweiser, which were very difficult to come by out in the bush, and gave them to me. They made sure I was off duty all night. They sat down in and around my foxhole and comforted me. And a Marine named Joe Fuller sang a song similar to "Thunder Road." Yes, the letter hurt. But it was great to be a Marine.

Still, beginning that night, the letter made me turn my back on God. Up to then, not even what I'd seen in 'Nam had shaken a faith that was nurtured in a devout Catholic family and those caring Catholic schools. But now a pattern of defiance and prayer evolved, and that begin to define my Catholicism. Pray and defy. That's what drove me. By "defy," I'm talking about some of the Ten Commandments. That's all I'm saying. It's between my priest confessors and me.

I drank the beers and went to sleep. The next day, I woke up feeling good, not even a hangover, and ready to roll.

Over the years, my relationship with God would fluctuate back and forth depending on the state of combat or a morally conflicting situation in which I might find myself. From my Marine Corps discharge through 1998, I would be a sincere, faithful, practicing Catholic, then slide into lapsed Catholicism, always caught in the conflict of self-autonomy, pride and defiance.

I would sin, confess, ask for forgiveness, be pardoned and sin again. My soul was in constant turmoil. But my psychosis and its related conditions would ultimately break my occasional resistance to God. Leading to deep self-examination, it would show me the Way, the Truth and the Life, with the help of Father Capodanno's memory and others.

When I was a youngster, the priests and brothers of the Sacred Heart taught me that we are in this world to love and to serve God. But even though I always dedicated my life's work to the service of God, I continued to be a contradiction unto myself.

On Dec. 13, I helped re-supply food and ammo to Hill 71, which was being manned by the First Platoon at the time. Along the way, I spotted 25 or 30 young Vietnamese males working the paddies. All were dressed in black pajamas. As I think back on it, I may have been the only one in that re-supply detail who made sense out of what I saw because I had patrolled the area frequently.

Something was up, I figured. During previous patrols, I'd seen no more than two or three old "papasans" working the paddies. Back at headquarters, I told the first authority figure I saw, my company sergeant, about what I'd seen. He said he'd pass it on to the company commander.

The defensive perimeter of Hill 71, close to a mile from battalion HQ, had two or three bunkers, and there was a large tent on the crest of the hill to house Marines not on duty. Generally, the area around 71 was considered secure.

But about 2 a.m. that night, the platoon sergeant woke us up with the news that Hill 71 was in deep trouble, under attack. My immediate reaction, facing what could have been my first firefight, was that our guys were in trouble and desperately needed help. I wasn't scared. The fate of the Marines and my friend Roland was uppermost in my mind. That's where all that training paid off.

I grabbed my fighting gear and four grenades. In the distance, we heard explosions and automatic and semiautomatic rifle fire. We were ready to rush out and help the First Platoon. But they didn't send us out of concern that we'd be walking into an ambush in the open rice paddies that led to Hill 71.

We were all frustrated and spent the rest of the night on full alert. The next morning, the situation report came in. Ten Marines had been killed, several more wounded, and the platoon had been overrun. Ten Popular Forces South Vietnamese soldiers assigned to the northern flank of the perimeter had slipped away before the assault, leaving the Marines undefended from that direction. Several weeks later, we got word that those ten soldiers were executed for desertion, shot in the head by their commanding officer.

I asked about PFC Guerrette's fate. Manning the point during the assault, he was the first to die when a recoilless rifle round penetrated his bunker. I volunteered to go ID the body, but someone told me, "Don, you don't want to do that."

In June 2006, I visited Roland's grave at Sts. Peter and Paul Cemetery in my hometown of Lewiston.

Over the next several days, we resumed patrolling the Ky Phu II and Thanmy Trung basin. Our squad was taking part in a CAP (Civilian Action Patrol) program, in which a squad went into a village, usually with a corpsman, to attend the sick and injured. We also did small patrols with the local Popular Forces troops. The idea was to display good will toward the populace.

While patrolling the Ky Phu II area one day, our fire team (part of a squad) spotted a lone Vietnamese woman approaching on a trail. She was wearing a veil that covered her nose and mouth.

To identify her, we stopped her and asked her to lift her veil. What we saw was horrifying -- a triangular, deep black hole where her nose should have been. She was a leper. We were all embarrassed and felt deeply sorry for her. Ever since then, when I hear the song "Painted Black" by the Rolling Stones, I think of her.

In Ky Phu II, I befriended two ten-year-old Vietnamese boys. They loved Marines. They gave us bottles of Coke and we paid them generously. One of the boys had been terribly burned by napalm on his face, chest and right arm.

In January 1967, Third Platoon found itself in a place called Dak To, centrally located in the rice-growing area of Vietnam, where we guarded a newly arrived artillery battery. We set up a defensive perimeter at night and patrolled during the day. During one patrol, as we crossed a rice paddy, the enemy opened up on us from a tree line to our right.

The squad starting running on the rice paddy dikes for the shelter of a tree line on our left flank. Midway through that run, I suddenly had severe and debilitating stomach cramps. I just *had* to stop and relieve myself right then and there as the rest of the squad ran around me and made it to the tree line. That left the enemy fire fully directed my way.

I did my thing, stood up, grabbed my rifle and sprinted to the tree line. I'll never forget the sight: my squad mates jumping, hollering and hooting, their arms waving me forward. And they were laughing hysterically.

"You crazy son of a bitch," one Marine shouted at me.

All I could say was, "When you gotta go, you gotta go."

About a week later, I identified the source of my stomach illness and constant diarrhea. I had tapeworms. Word got out and from then on, I was known as "the worm." Later that week, a doctor told me I also had amoebic dysentery. The afflictions weren't bad enough to put me out of service, but I was put on medication for both problems, long enough with the tapeworm pills to keep up with the larvae cycle going on in my guts. I probably contacted the tapeworms from walking in muddy rice paddies and the amoebic dysentery from drinking ground water.

In early February of 1967, Mike Company was walking along a trail at the edge of a ridgeline flanked on the left by a large open expanse of rice paddies. I was at the rear of the column with the Third Squad, Third Platoon. A single shot rang out. That brought the whole column to a halt.

Within minutes, a request filtered back to Third Platoon. The company point man had been shot and killed in a small opening along the trail, and the CO was asking for volunteers to retrieve the fallen Marine. Three Marines had already volunteered and they needed one more.

I volunteered to be the fourth. It was the right and honorable thing to do. The Marine Corps prides itself on leaving no one behind, dead or wounded, and I felt the relatives and friends of this fallen hero would need closure. They sent me to the head of the column, where the CO briefed us. He told us where to find the body, and made it clear that we'd be exposed to enemy fire.

We dropped our packs and, carrying only our M-14 rifles, rushed into the clearing. Instantly, we came under enemy fire. Rounds were flying all around us. At least two zipped by my right arm near my armpit.

When we reached the lifeless hero, I recognized him as a Marine I had met at breakfast that morning. We had introduced ourselves to one another. I recalled that he put ketchup on his scrambled eggs, something I had never seen before. Now here he was, dead and lifeless, shot through the heart.

His mouth was agape and his tongue pointed straight out. He had blond hair and his baby blue eyes were open. Nineteen years old and dead to this world. We each grabbed a limb -- I had his left arm -- and we raced back to the relative security of the company, under fire the whole time.

We had done it. We had brought back one of our own and no one else had been hit. After covering his body with a poncho liner, I went back to the end of the column. Before long, shots rang out to our left, from the rice paddy. One shot at a time, like a sniper again. Marines had already taken a protective position from the enemy force on the left because that's where the sniper's fire had came from, not to mention the fire directed our way from the right when we recovered the body. So we were getting it from both sides -- a classic ambush.

Even worse, word filtered back that the Navy corpsman who was tending to the dying had himself been shot in the head by the rice paddy sniper. Not long after that, a rocket team and a squad circled behind the sniper and took him out with a rocket. The sniper had been using a single-shot .50 caliber rifle with a scope that gave him unusual accuracy as well as tremendous killing power.

After we silenced the sniper, the company commander called for an air strike on the enemy position to our right. A Marine F-4 Phantom jet came flying in at treetop level and dropped a 250-pound bomb. But he dropped it prematurely, shaking up the whole company. The bomb hit a Vietnamese hut 50 to 100 meters from us, wiping out the family inside.

Several minutes later word came back to the Third Platoon that one of the victims was a 2- or 3-year-old boy whose head had been severed from his body. That was a major blow that no amount of training could have prepared us to absorb. The sorrow and sense of shame hung heavy over all of us. The innocent, those whom we were protecting, had become our victims.

A day or two later, Mike Company was ordered to the southwestern base of a large hill near Dak To. At that time, my foxhole partner was a kid we all called "Schmiddy," about 5'10" and a little paunchy, with grayish rheumy eyes and thinning hair.

After we established a defensive perimeter, Marines started firing 105-millimeter artillery rounds from the top of the hill to our right toward a hamlet 200 meters to our left. Schmiddy and I were sitting on the edge of a dike and we tried to follow the projectiles as they flew overhead. If you twisted your head from right to left in quick fashion, you could sometimes pick out the blur of the projectiles. At one point, we heard the boom of the cannon, heard a low whishing sound and a big splash and slurp in the rice paddy nearby. It was a "short round," and it was sticking out of the mud about 50 feet away. All we could do was laugh, then notify command of the unexploded round.

But reflecting on our lucky escape, I developed a terrible premonition. I felt sure that we were going to get hit that night and that I would be a casualty.

As it was getting dark, about 7 p.m., Third Squad was dispatched to that hamlet 200 yards away to set up a night ambush. Intelligence thought the hamlet held a large cache of rice, and that Viet Cong and North Vietnamese troops would be collecting their supper. They were right.

As soon as he entered the outer edge of the little ville, our point man made contact. Shots were exchanged, and then stopped. We pulled back about 50 yards and waited for orders. Five or ten minutes later, the command post told us to proceed. We headed into a nearby ditch to set up.

A machine gunner and his "A gunner," an assistant who carried nearly 1,000 rounds of ammo, set up their M-60 to the left of Schmiddy and I. With most of the squad set up to our left, we were on the right, with two Marines to the right and rear of us.

It was drizzling and cool, a bit foggy. The time was about 8:20 p.m. We had been placed on 50 percent alert. I took the first watch and Schmiddy would relieve me at 9 p.m. Beyond that, we planned on doing two-hour watches until the break of dawn.

About 8:40, the artillery battery on the hill behind us suddenly fired illumination rounds over our position, causing our helmets, faces and ponchos to glisten. What the hell was going on? Our position had been compromised for no good reason. We yelled at the squad leader to alert the command post about the foul-up. Word came back that we were to stay there.

At 9, Schmiddy relieved me. I noticed that he wasn't wearing his flak jacket or helmet. I had mine on, as it was quite chilly out. I walked back about 10 feet from Schmiddy's position and laid down with my rifle in my right hand, not ready to go to 50 percent alert quite yet.

Within a minute, a series of explosions rocked the ground all around us. At least six grenades had been thrown into our position. It took a second or two before I felt a hot burning sensation from the shrapnel. Then I sensed warm blood dripping down from my face and my upper right arm. My right foot ached and throbbed and there was a deep wound in the center of my chest.

Shrapnel had entered my chest where the flak jacket was open a little bit at the top. To this day, I'm absolutely certain that my helmet and flak jacket saved my life. I rolled over and tried to fire my M-14 into the darkness where I thought the enemy might be lurking. But it wouldn't fire; the explosion had put it out of commission.

I looked for Schmiddy and saw that he was lying forward, face down. He was breathing very slowly and I could hear gurgling sounds every time he breathed. I crawled over to him. He was unconscious.

Then I crawled to my left to the machine gun position. Both Marines were unconscious and wounded. Fearing that they would overrun us, I got on my knees, grabbed the M-60 and pulled back the bolt to make sure it was loaded.

Several minutes went by before Navy Corpsman "Doc" Vacarro showed up. He was from Boston and he was a good friend. Schmiddy had been hit hardest, so Doc treated him first. Then he tended to the machine gunner and his mate. The machine gunner had taken a grenade blast to the face and was blind. After several more minutes, Doc treated me for my wounds.

Sergeant Lewis "Buddy" Ford and other Marines who had arrived in a relief column helped me walk back to the command post. A medevac helicopter arrived in about 30 minutes. The wounded -- I think there were six of us -- took a direct flight to the U.S.S. Repose hospital ship.

At triage, they removed my clothes and examined me, then put me in a secondary care unit for the time being. Before long, they x-rayed me. I had multiple fragment wounds to the face, chest and right arm, and a triple compound fracture of the fourth toe on my right foot.

The shrapnel in my chest was lodged two or three millimeters from my ascending aorta -- a close call. They wheeled me into surgery, arranged me in the fetal position, and gave me a spinal. My body jerked as the needle penetrated between the vertebrae. It was intensely painful -- a hot, throbbing, electric pain up and down my spine.

After a few seconds, I became numb from the neck down to my feet. I could feel nothing other than my face. I couldn't even feel myself breathing. I panicked a bit and they injected a sedative, which deadened the anxiety.

Looking in an overhead mirror, I could see the doctor (his last name was Glass) probing in my chest for the shrapnel. But he couldn't remove it because it was too close to the ascending aorta, and he didn't want to risk bursting it. Next he cleaned and sewed my facial wounds. Then he attended to the broken toe and right arm. I was on my way to Olangapo in the Philippines on the hospital ship.

On the trip, a week or so later, I visited my friend Schmiddy in intensive care. He still had not regained consciousness. I learned that the shrapnel wounds to the back of the head had penetrated his brain, and shrapnel had penetrated his lungs and heart. Several weeks later I heard that he didn't make it.

Olangopo was a well-known port of call, where hospital ships docked routinely. The wounded and the ships' crews spent a lot of time relaxing in Olangopo, where the girls were pretty, the booze was cheap and they had great shows in the evening.

It was May 1967 and we were operating in an area of northwestern South Vietnam called "Arizona" or the "Badlands" because so many Marines had been killed there. The company marched into a village in a VC-controlled area. There was carnage everywhere. All inhabitants had been killed, some mutilated and tortured.

Our squad entered a hooch. Lying on the floor was a young, beautiful South Vietnamese woman. On her left side lay an infant -- a baby boy about one year old. Both were dead. Someone had ripped apart her pajamas top. She was naked from the waist down.

The VC had taken a 1 ½-inch-diameter bamboo pole, sharpened at one end and impaled it in her private parts until the pole reached her bowels. She had died a terrible death. That scene justified my presence in Vietnam. Communism was indeed evil, and that's how we saw it. Over time, my attitude toward the war never changed. I was prepared to argue with any and all who challenged the propriety of our involvement in Vietnam.

In late June 1967, our platoon was ordered to guard a bridge on Route 1, the main highway between Chu Lai and Da Nang. Across the road from our bivouac was an expanse of rice paddies about a half-mile square. At the end of the rice paddies were the rivers that drained them.

Our squad was to patrol in the paddies up to the edge of the river, almost a half-mile away. We were told not to cross the river under any circumstances, as a large contingent of North Vietnamese troops were known to be on the other side. We left the platoon perimeter about 9 a.m. on a hot day. Third Squad had brought along a machine gunner. I don't recall his name, but it was Polish. I had told him earlier not to be a hero and that if we got into a fight, he should seek cover.

Well, for some reason I don't remember, we did cross that river. As soon as we climbed the opposite riverbank, we took intense fire, and we were pinned down pretty badly. After a couple minutes, the machine gunner got up, stood on the edge of the riverbank, began to fire his M-60 and hollered, "Come and get me, mother fuckers!"

Right away, I heard a muffled sound and looked over. He was 15 feet away, lying on his back, shot between the eyes. Another Marine had been shot in the ankle. It was time to retreat. Carrying the dead and wounded, we returned to the platoon perimeter. Lesson learned: No more John Wayne hero stuff.

Then came a break of sorts. In late July, the Fifth Marines threw a party in a large tent. There were pallets upon pallets of Budweiser. Two companies not doing perimeter security were invited, and Mike Company was one of them. I had two or three beers, and watched some 250 Marines dancing and gyrating to the sounds of Bob Dylan's "Rainy Day Woman." After months of fighting in the jungle and rice paddies, it's what we needed -- a taste of home and being young and partying.

Then in early August, the Third Platoon was patrolling an area heavily infested by NVA regulars. One day, we were walking down a trail, alert to the max because we could just *feel* the enemy all around us.

I was about the tenth Marine from the rear of the column. Something made me look to the right and I spotted the heads of two NVA soldiers. They were kneeling or sitting behind a downed tree and they were pointing weapons at us. I swung around, took aim at their heads and fired 12 to 14 bullets on full automatic (we switched from the M-14 rifle to the M-16 in May of that year).

I thought I hit both of them. They didn't fire at us, so I think I caught them by surprise. They both disappeared from sight and I was quite sure I had gotten them.

The column came to a stop and we got into a defensive position, kneeling and facing both flanks in alternative fashion because it could have been an ambush. The platoon commander ran back and ordered me to check it out with my four-man fire team (I had been promoted to corporal, E-4). Slowly, we approached the spot where I'd seen them.

But no bodies, no blood trails. Apparently I didn't hit them. But they did abandon their SKS semiautomatic rifles and packs. The packs contained articles of clothing, rice, ammunition and other items.

We brought the booty back to the lieutenant, who ordered us to share the "goods," including the rifles, if we wanted to carry them. There were plenty of takers. I took a small tin can of oil/grease that had Chinese writing on it. I still have it today. As a final word, the lieutenant shook my hand and said, "You probably saved a few Marines. Thanks." And the patrol resumed.

Mid-August 1967. Mike Company was deployed somewhere in the I Corps area in the northwest. We rarely were told where we were going. They did tell us, however, that our mission was to sweep through a known Viet Cong village -- a 100 percent kill zone. We were ordered to kill every living animal we saw and to burn all the hooches in the village.

The orders got us talking among ourselves. Did 100 percent kill zone mean killing everyone we spotted? Would we kill an old papasan riding a water buffalo unarmed? No way. Would we kill unarmed civilians or women and children? Absolutely not. Out of the question. Would we burn the hooches to deprive the enemy comfort and cover? Absolutely.

So we swept through the ville. Not a shot was fired and we burned all the dwellings. I recall thinking, "Man, I'd be pissed off if someone burned my home." The only living creature we saw was a humongous water buffalo, which the rocket launcher team dispatched quickly. Most Marines were quite exuberant over the kill. Some were saddened. I was neutral about it -- no different than bagging a white-tailed deer or a moose.

Chesuncook

From the ville, the company formed a column and began marching west on a trail headed for our night bivouac. Third Platoon once again was "tail-end Charlie" and Third Squad was the tail of the tail end, providing rear security.

About five minutes after we cleared the village perimeter, a machine gun on a hill to our right rear opened up on us. We all turned to the right and fired at a cave-like structure that was the source of the fire. That brought our Third Platoon machine gun team on a run, and they started firing into the hollow.

But we didn't seem to have any effect. Suddenly, to our rear, on our left flank, about eight Viet Cong or North Vietnamese soldiers blasted us with what sounded like AK-47s. Some of us turned 180 degrees to suppress this fire. The company was moving out. Half-crouched, we followed as best we could, and the fire from both flanks ceased. After maybe 150 feet, we were out of the cave machine gunner's sight.

But there was more, much more. This time, it was intense fire from our left flank. As we fired at their muzzle flashes, I glanced back down the trail and saw a lone female trailing the company about 75 yards away. She was wearing black pajamas. She did not have a weapon.

The company began to move out again and the firing stopped momentarily. I kept my eye on the woman who was keeping pace with us. Suddenly she stopped, and the firing broke out again on our left, even more frenzied than before.

We were all on our knees to minimize exposure. For some reason, I broke a cardinal rule that I had taught all the new guys to help them survive: Don't overexpose yourself and try to be a hero. Unwisely, I stood up in clear sight of the enemy, which attracted most of their gunfire. I returned fire as fast as I could, reloading and laying a base of fire.

I figured that if someone didn't establish what they called "fire superiority" in training, we were going to have KIA. I fired over 200 rounds, and must have had several hundred rounds directed my way. And I didn't get a scratch.

In fact, no one got hit, a miracle in itself. It had to be some sort of divine providence. The enemy was well hidden in the jungle. The squad was not. We were standing on a wide-open trail when we got hit, and the company commander got us walking forward. And for some reason, I remained the only one standing. Very stupid. Everyone else in the squad was either kneeling or in the prone position when the firing started.

Finally, the firing subsided and we got moving. I looked back and saw that female again. I grabbed the radio and told the company commander that I thought she was marking the end of the column to help the ambushers. He ordered us to "take her out." I passed the order down the line, but the Marine at the end of the column refused to shoot her.

Since I was the senior enlisted man in the rear, it was up to me to do the dirty work. I walked to the rear of the column, raised my rifle to my right shoulder, aimed at her chest area, and did a double take. She was holding a small child in her left arm, nestled on her chest.

That was the first time I saw the child, who looked to be two or three years old. Now I had to think. Staring at her, I suddenly envisioned a fresco of Mary, the Mother of God, holding the baby Jesus in her left arm. Questions raced through my mind. Should I shoot her and leave a child motherless? Suppose I shot and hit them both accidentally? Then what?

While I pondered, the woman and child melted back into the bush. Thank God. I returned to my position and we resumed our march. After I took four or five steps, the Marine in front of me, an old-timer named Drake Willoughby, turned to me and said, "I was watching you when you stood up" and fired at the enemy.

He said he saw numerous tracer rounds fly by my head and he thought I was a dead man. When I heard that, I knew I should have been. For the first time in Vietnam, I got scared. My knees buckled under me, and I began to shake and ended up kneeling on the ground. I crossed myself and said the "Our Father" and thanked Him for sparing my life.

I had been a lapsed Catholic since the previous December when I got that Dear John letter. I had turned on God and was defiant. Now I was praying and thanking Him for my very survival.

The company marched on and after about three hours, we set up a night defensive perimeter. I got word that the woman I had almost shot had entered the perimeter with the child and asked to participate in the Chieu Hoi program, which offered amnesty to former VC. Once again, I prayed to Our Lord and thanked His mother Mary. I had almost shot an innocent woman.

The incident resurfaced 33 years later, after I had recovered from my psychosis and its delusions. In the summer of 2000, I looked out into the field behind my home at a pine tree some 75 yards away, and I saw the Vietnamese woman holding her child. I knew it was just my imagination; it was just a pine tree. But for two or three days, every time I looked out there, I "saw" the woman and her child.

That shook me up a lot, so I spoke to my local priest about the incident back in Vietnam. He told me not to dwell on it and added that many bad things happen in wartime. I thanked him and walked away feeling somehow complete after all those years.

September 4, 1967. 9:30 a.m. The hot topic in Mike Company was the plight of Delta Company, First Battalion, Fifth Marines. Delta had been ambushed that morning by a vastly superior NVA force. They were in danger of being overrun and massacred. We knew them as the Dying Delta because they were always "in the shit" and suffered a lot of KIAs every time they engaged the enemy.

Mike Company and Kilo Company were ordered to help relieve them. We knew we were in for a big fight, with at least a regiment of NVA in the Que Son Valley several miles west of Tam Ky. Some of us would almost certainly be killed. I was a "short-timer," as were many Marines in the Third Platoon. We were due to rotate back to the states in a month or so. That bothered us, and some talked about it right then and there.

But Sgt. Lewis "Buddy" Ford picked up on that and said, "Hey guys, Delta's in deep trouble. Marines need our help." That did it. Everyone clammed up and got ready. When we were ordered to saddle up, we headed over to several helicopters, where we got the word that we were likely to be entering a very hot LZ (landing zone).

That got our attention, of course. The ride from battalion headquarters took only a few minutes. When we got there, we linked up with Kilo Company without incident.

It was a hot humid day, at least 94 degrees by 10 a.m. As soon as we started marching, we perspired profusely. As usual, we had no idea where we had landed or where we were headed. All we knew was that Delta was in trouble somewhere in the Que Son Valley, and we were going to relieve them.

And we were in for a hard march. The scuttlebutt us grunts picked up was that all the LZs closer to the Dying Delta were real hot and any attempt to drop the companies in those areas could have meant extremely heavy casualties.

After a couple hours marching, K Company took a position on our left. We crossed a small river and followed a trail that meandered through a few villages. At one ville, we stopped to see what sort of intelligence we could get from the inhabitants and to rest and have a bite to eat. We then resumed our march, having learned nothing new.

After three to three and a half hours of marching, the company column came to a halt, with Third Platoon in the center. First Platoon had the company point and Second was tail-end Charlie. At one point, the order came to switch places with the Second. As they walked by, I was sitting along the trail with my fire team.

I was with Bill Paul, Frank Miller and others. I was frustrated and vented: "Jesus Christ, fuck this shit. What a freakin place!" But just as I said it, I looked up and there was Father Capodanno looking down at me. He had heard me clearly. And on his face was a kind look of understanding. He knew the grunt Marine Corps language.

I'll never forget the man. Father Capodanno stood about 5'11". He was about 170 pounds, had a gray crew cut, and appeared to be quite sinewy. He wore jungle fatigues and had the Cross of Christ on both lapels. He was unarmed. Before that day, I had seen him give general absolution to the company Catholics before another major encounter.

Another time when I saw him walking around, a Marine told me he was a grunt's ideal chaplain and was highly respected throughout the Fifth Marines. He had a reputation for going to the assistance of young Marines when the going got tough in battle.

But now I felt terrible. Here I was, a former altar boy who served mass at St. Peter and Paul's Church in Lewiston for seven years, and I was talking like that! I apologized for my comments. He didn't say anything, but his face told me he understood and forgave my trespass.

Then he sat and visited with us for a couple minutes. There was something peaceful in the man's countenance. After he smoked a cigarette with us, he got up and walked down the line toward the front of the company. That was the last time I saw him alive.

After a few minutes, we got the order to move out. The time was about 2:15 p.m. As Third Platoon entered the jungle canopy, I noticed a few hooches along the trail. We'd been walking for about 15 minutes when our world suddenly turned very loud and dangerous. We could hear intense firing to our right front. There must have been thousands of rounds fired, including heavy automatic weapons from our rear.

They knew exactly where we were, front and back. It was an ambush, and there were lots of them. Four or five of us in the absolute rear guard zone got prone in a hurry and returned fire, aiming at numerous muzzle flashes as the rounds whizzed cracked and snapped all around us -- trying to protect Mike Company from the rear. At the same time, I kept my eye on Third Platoon ahead of us, ready to move when they did. If we didn't follow them, we could get cut off and perhaps annihilated.

Someone popped a red smoke grenade -- it had to be the NVA -- dead in the center of the platoon position. As it happens, red smoke is how you pinpoint the enemy. Moments later, a Marine helicopter gunship flying at tree top level opened up on the Third Platoon. Rounds tore into tree leaves and limbs around us, sounding like heavy rain when you're in a tent. It was some bad shit.

Right away, the platoon commander popped a yellow smoke grenade to identify us as friendlies. Man, taking fire from the rear and from your own air support really made you pucker. Then, after the platoon commander talked to the chopper pilot, the gunship shifted its target and fired at the enemy. That gave us a break, and we all moved out at double pace. We had to join up with our sister platoons, which were taking withering fire, lest we be cut off and surrounded.

After a minute or so of double-timing, we came to a halt. In front of us was an open field. We gathered ourselves, and as the first few Marines began to run, mortar rounds started to fall. No doubt about it, the NVA was trying to cut us off from the rest of the company.

We crossed three and four at a time. Being in the rear, Third Squad was the last to cross. As we sprinted across the open space, several mortar rounds exploded in our midst. Hitting the deck, I felt the sting of flying particles penetrating the right side of my neck. I felt some blood with my hand, but it wasn't serious.

I got up and ran the next 60 or 80 feet without further incident until I reached the relative safety of the rest of Third Platoon. We'd been told to set up a defensive perimeter. Our squad was on the side of a hill away from the most brutal fighting. We were told to watch for K Company, who would be joining us from that direction.

What happened is that First Platoon walked into an ambush and Second Platoon had gone to their aid and was pinned down by extraordinary volumes of enemy gunfire. Two-thirds of the company was in danger of being overrun. We were nearly surrounded. The relentless gunfire hit crescendos of unimaginable volume

Third Platoon was in a semi-circle, hunkered down awaiting orders from the company commander. We hadn't been told to dig in yet. On the flank where we were, we didn't see any enemy to fire at. We watched for K Company, but didn't see it. I think they finally showed up somewhere around dawn.

About 3:30 p.m., the company commander, 1st Lt. John Murray, called for a tear gas drop on the enemy line, which was getting closer all the time. Many Marines were dead or otherwise out of commission and we were in dire need of help. Those of us who had gas masks were ordered to put them on. Then the chopper swooped in and dropped the CS gas right on top of us.

The gas masks were unbearable -- hot, sweaty and stifling. I couldn't see out of it as my eyes were stinging with sweat. Finally, I yanked off the mask and my vision cleared up right away. The tear gas burned but at least I could see.

After the tear gas drop, I don't recall any more help from helicopter gunships until the next morning. There were just too many bullets flying around -- enough to shoot down any chopper.

But that didn't mean the skies were empty. About 4:30 p.m., an A-6 attack jet screamed down at the enemy position, maybe 80 to 120 meters from us. And right away, the NVA responded with anti-aircraft guns. I could hear the rhythmic pumping of those guns and saw the projectiles slam into the aircraft. Why it wasn't shot down, I'll never know.

But I do know the A-6 dropped a high explosive bomb where the anti-aircraft guns appeared to be. The pilot made a second pass, and while still taking fire, he dropped a napalm bomb on the anti-aircraft position. The air filled with rolling balls of fire, and we were ecstatic. Almost in unison we stood up and hollered, "Get some!" The enemy guns were silent. The jet made a third pass and strafed the NVA infantry positions. Finally, the enemy fire directed at us began to abate.

I took my M-16 and scurried over to the opposite side of the perimeter to share a hole with a close friend named Corporal Moisky from Philadelphia. He told me the NVA soldiers were using three- or four-foot-high bushes to camouflage their approach. So we fired into the nearest bushes. But right away, my M-16 jammed.

Frustrated and angry, I scoured the company perimeter for weapons that had been left lying around. I picked up three other rifles, but they were also jammed and worthless. Finally, the fourth one I tried was in good working order. I fired a few more rounds and went back to my original position just in time for another rising burst of enemy fire.

Mortar rounds began to hit inside our position, which was about 60 meters in diameter. The corpsman brought two wounded Marines over the crest of the hill and put them right behind us, where they lay in pain and agony. Another mortar round fell and hit both of them with shrapnel.

The corpsman patched them up and moved them to a spot to the left of us, where another mortar round hit them a third time. Their moaning and screaming got worse. They were patched up again, and moved to a 250-pound bomb crater where they spent the night. I didn't think they were going to make it.

The order came down to dig in, which meant we were here for the long haul. Beginning to dig with my entrenching tool, I was bent over at the waist. Then came a tremendous blast and complete darkness. In a short time -- I don't know how long -- I regained consciousness and realized I had been hit in the back.

My lower spine ached and there was a hot searing pain on the upper right side of my back. It hurt to breathe. I thought my lungs might have been punctured. Bill Paul crawled over and began to slice my shirt open with a K-Bar, which was a prized possession of many a Marine. Much shorter than a bayonet, it had a smooth edge and was easy to sharpen. Bill was trying to patch me up.

But in his rush and anxiety, he stuck the knife directly into the upper wound. I yelled, "Jesus Christ, Bill, what are you doing?" I could see he was nervous as hell, and for some reason that made me laugh. It was just plain funny, but of course it was nervous laughter. Before long, Paul and Frank Miller were laughing, too. Comic relief in a bad, bad situation. Frank would be killed in Operation Swift three days later.

Bill and Frank hollered "corpsman up!" which brought one over the crest of the hill. He wrapped my chest and back with a large chest bandage, then helped me walk back to the bomb crater, which was maybe 25 feet across, where I spent the rest of the night with 30 or so other wounded Marines. We would have made a great mortar target.

The firing went on at a steady pace until about 6:30 p.m., when an old C-47 gunship appeared overhead and circled our perimeter firing its "mini-guns," electronically operated machine guns that put out an unbelievable amount of bullets. It was known far and wide as "Puff the Magic Dragon," after the Peter, Paul and Mary song. The noise sounded like a foghorn or maybe an elephant farting. That was our best hope because since the gas drop by the chopper, no other helicopters dared enter the killing zone.

When things got to their worst, the enemy had penetrated our lines and they were about 25 to 35 meters from the bomb crater. The company was pretty much in the open and the NVA were concealed in what amounted to an advancing tree line using cut bushes as their camouflage. I was pretty confident that the Marines still in fighting condition could protect us wounded guys at all costs.

I knew I might die, but I was going to go down fighting. There was an awful lot of agonized moaning in the crater. One of the things that crossed my mind was that it was over for me. But if we survived the night, I'd probably be heading home in a few more weeks.

As it turned out, Puff the Magic Dragon slowed the enemy fire down considerably. But that didn't mean we were in the clear. About 8 p.m. a corporal came by, asked how I was doing, and said he needed my weapon or any ammunition I might have on me. I told him that when I was hit I left my rifle and ammo with the other guys.

The company was running out of ammo and we couldn't get resupplied because this area was too hot -- and too dark -- for choppers. Several minutes later, the corporal came back and said the CO had ordered everyone to fix bayonets. He expected the NVA to try to overrun us. It could be a massacre in the making.

And there I was, hopeless -- no rifle, no bayonet, no K-bar, no weapons of any kind. Still, I was ready to fight. About that time, we got word that Father Capodanno had been killed. I said the "Our Father," the Catholic version of "The Lord's Prayer." Back in boot camp, we sang it every evening. I asked God to forgive me for all my sins, to have mercy on my soul and to bring me to everlasting life. I prayed the same for Father Capodanno. I asked the Lord to take Father Cap and all those who had fallen that day into his embrace. At that point, I wasn't really afraid, but I felt a deep hatred for the NVA for what it had done to the company and, more importantly, to Father Cap.

The night wore on and I fell asleep. There was no more fighting. The NVA had quietly slipped back into the jungle as they had been too bloodied to continue, apparently. The next morning, as they led me to the medevac area, I counted 16 poncho liners covering bodies. I asked one Marine where Father Cap was and he pointed to him.

All I saw were his boots and a poncho covering his body. I was about to remove the poncho to have a last look at him, and someone said, "Don't do it, he was just about cut in half." I later learned through Father Daniel Mode's book, "The Grunt Padre," that Father Cap had been shot 27 times in the back and the back of the head.

With that, I walked away and wondered why he had been killed. He was not a combat Marine. He didn't have to be there with us. I had assumed that he stayed within the relative safety of the company command post. I was wrong.

Mike Company had taken heavy casualties. Fourteen Marines, one corpsman and Father Capodanno had been killed, with 37 wounded. We lost more than one-third of the company's strength, all in six hours of fighting, and that was only the first day of what they were calling Operation Swift. As a grunt, I didn't get much intel, but I did learn that a division of NVA soldiers had entered or were near the Que Son Valley area to influence the elections that were to be held in September. It was the 5th Marine Regiment's job to drive them out.

Several other companies had also been bloodied during that first day. Before I left the battle area while talking to Vern Randolph, I couldn't help but notice an eerie quietness that had come over the company. Everyone seemed to be dumbfounded and deeply affected by the deaths, particularly that of Father Capodanno. The loss of the priest would touch many Marines. I've spoken with at least four Marines who were on Operation Swift, one of whom killed the NVA machine gunner and his partner who had gunned down Father Cap.

Father Mode wrote eloquently about the effect that Father Cap's death had on many, including high-ranking officers and other chaplains, for the rest of their lives. I only wish I could have died in his place. And I mean that. A lot of guys would have given up their lives willingly to save the Father, the reason being in part what St. John the Evangelist said, "There is no greater love than that shown by one who lays down his life for another." The message is always love.

I was on the first medevac out. As the chopper lifted off, Vernon Randolph was standing there looking at me. He had been my best friend in Vietnam. He was my protector, and I was his teacher. I had taught him everything I knew about how to survive combat.

I arrived in Vietnam in October 1966 and Vernon arrived the next April. He was assigned to my squad. As it turned out, some of the guys liked to pick on me because I wasn't a particularly large or strong person. Vernon -- tall, strong and fast with his fists -- became my instant friend and we developed a deep love for one another.

He protected me from those who wanted to fight me and I taught him what I knew about surviving the war. I taught him to stay undercover as often as he could, not to volunteer for certain death assignments, like going out to retrieve a fallen Marine (even though I'd done just that), assaulting a machine gun position or otherwise exposing yourself voluntarily to hostile enemy gunfire. I taught him to keep low and not be a hero. I also taught him the intricacies of calling in mortar rounds on enemy positions and how to communicate with helicopter gunships.

As the helicopter clawed its way into the air, Vernon reached his right hand up and waved and I waved back to him. That was the last I saw of Vernon Randolph. On Feb. 7, 1968, in a heroic action, he was killed in the line of duty. All I heard was that he had volunteered to place himself under enemy fire to retrieve a major weapon that had been abandoned behind enemy lines unintentionally.

After I averted my eyes from Vern, I lowered my head and felt the presence of angels around me. I was overwhelmed by emotion. I thanked God for allowing me to survive and told him I would use the rest of my life, to the best of my ability, for the betterment of mankind. I wanted to help create a better society, to help families become better families, to help individuals become better individuals, all in God's name and according to His plans. To help the needy, the oppressed and the forlorn. To obtain justice for all. Sounds pretty idealistic, I know, but that's what I perceive to be God's will for me.

As I think this book shows, I tried to live up to that pledge.

In 1980, I read the first public account -- at least the first one I'd seen -- of Mike Company's predicament on Sept. 14, 1967. I learned that Father Capodanno had been awarded the Congressional Medal of Honor. Also awarded the Medal of Honor was Lawrence Peters, the Second Platoon sergeant. It was written up in the American Legion magazine. In the year 2000, "The Grunt Padre," written by Father Mode, celebrated Father Cap's life. It is a must read.

(Briefly, Father Vincent Robert Capodanno, Jr., was born in 1929 of Italian immigrant parents in Staten Island, N.Y. He was the youngest of 10 children and was 37 years old when he was martyred for Christ, his country and his Marines. He was trained as a Maryknoll priest and served in Taiwan before being assigned to the Seventh Marines in Vietnam in the spring of 1965. After his tour of duty was over, he asked for and was given an extension, continuing to serve the Fifth Marines as well as the Seventh Regiment. His death had a deep and profound impact on all the surviving Marines.)

After leaving the battle area, we flew into battalion headquarters and I was taken to the aid station. The surgeon removed my bloody shirt and asked me to lay face down on a table. He apologized that there were no painkillers available -- no morphine, no aspirin, nothing. So fierce were the battles underway that they had all been consumed. I had no choice but to bear it.

As I bit down on a rubber mouthpiece, the surgeon cut into the flesh of my back with his scalpel. I began to sweat and muttered a shaky "mmmm, mmmm." A hot and searing pain increased in intensity as the scalpel cut through the flesh around my lower spine. That was the lower wound -- one-quarter inch from my spine. He removed the shrapnel and placed it in a clear plastic container.

Then he proceeded to the upper wound. As he cut, more red-hot searing pain. I bit down and squeezed the sides of the table. My head was tilted to the right. A young Marine happened to be walking by. He looked over, turned ashen white and vomited at the sight of the blood. I thought to my self, "Jesus, I must have been hit pretty bad."

After bandaging my wounds, the Doc gave me the container with the shrapnel he had taken from my lower back as a war souvenir. The shrapnel in the upper wound could not be removed because doing so would have caused additional muscle damage.

That afternoon, they flew me to regimental headquarters, where I boarded another chopper for Da Nang first and then to a hospital in Chu Lai. Waiting for the chopper, I counted 275 to 300 bodies laying next to the tarmac, all wrapped in body bags. I thought, "Fifth Marines is really in a major battle here."

I learned that some 500 enemy soldiers had tangled with Mike Company. Later accounts would put it at a much higher figure, noting that the company had walked into the rear guard of a full regiment. Considering the NVA's anti-aircraft guns, I figured the estimate of a regiment was probably accurate.

For the flight to DaNang, I boarded a CH-53 chopper along with 27 dead Marines and six wounded Marines. Some of the bodies had begun to decompose and some were going through the saponification process. Most were black, gray or blue; some were yellow. That happens when a corpse begins to turn into a soap-like substance caused by extended exposure to humidity, water and warmth. Saponification is derived from the French word for soap, "sapon."

We were at about 3,000 feet when the helicopter's rotors suddenly lost their lifting power, or at least that's how it felt. As it descended rapidly, I remember being not scared, just resigned to my fate. We landed in a rice paddy with a thud. The co-pilot grabbed a screwdriver, climbed up to the rotor blade base and did something that apparently fixed the problem.

We lifted off, and now I was fearful, but we made it. Why wasn't I that afraid in combat? The answer -- and a lot of other combat vets will tell you the same thing -- is that serious shooting contact with the enemy usually leads immediately to acceptance of almost certain death. You see it in some soldiers -- the "thousand-yard stare" that made you neutral to the prospect of death and made your eyes vacant.

When the chopper started to drop out of the sky, I was resigned to the fate of death. When it landed safely, my resignation turned to joy. But then we had to fly back up there, and that scared me. It's hard to explain. I guess you had to be there.

In Chu Lai, I checked into the hospital and I found three squad mates -- Gary Wells, Rodney Kuvass and a guy named Smith. All three had been hit about the same time I got hit, and Wells was wounded by the same mortar round that sidelined me.

Not long after we got there, a corpsman who gave us our penicillin shots appeared to be overdoing the butt slapping bit that medics do before they inject you with a hypodermic. We all noticed it, but let it go, at least for the time being.

That night, all four of us, with bandages on various parts of our bodies, snuck out of the hospital ward and headed to a bar operated by the Americal Division of the U.S. Army. We were in our pajamas. We didn't know what type of reception we'd get and wondered if we'd get into a bar fight because we were Marines. But no, guys came up to us and shook our hands and we all drank beer for about two hours. We were their honored guests.

We returned to the ward, where they gave us sleeping medications. About 11 p.m., there was a major commotion that woke up everyone in the room. Someone was yelling for the officer of the day. Apparently, the corpsman had started to take sexual advantage of a big black wounded Marine who he'd sedated, and the guy reacted by clobbering him over the head with a crutch.

He had been caught in the act. The corpsman was subsequently arrested and, we all hoped, convicted and sent to perform hard labor somewhere. Two days later, on the USS Repose hospital ship, we saw him in the brig.

Eventually, we put out to sea for Olangopo, Philippines, a rest and recovery area for the wounded. On arriving in port, I was playing blackjack with a bunch of guys when I was taken aside and told that my father had suffered a severe heart attack. I was heading home. The trouble was that I felt being wounded a second time had triggered the heart attack. I felt guilty as hell, and that would play a part in my psychotic episode in 1998.

Congressional Medal of Honor
awarded to
Vincent R. Capodanno
Second Lieutenant
United States Navy
Born: February 13, 1929
Casualty on September 4, 1967
In QUANG TIN, SOUTH VIETNAM

The Congressional Medal of Honor is the highest award for Valor in action against an enemy, which can be bestowed upon an individual serving in the Armed Services of the United States. Jim Capodanno, Father Capodanno's brother, received the Medal of Honor, which was awarded posthumously, for his brother Vincent on January 7, 1969.

The citation reads: "For conspicuous gallantry and intrepidity at the risk of his life above and beyond the call of duty as Chaplain of the 3d Battalion, in connection with operations against enemy forces. In response to reports that the 2d Platoon of M Co was in danger of being overrun by a massed enemy assaulting force, Lt. Capodanno left the relative safety of the company command post and ran through an open area raked with fire, directly to the beleaguered platoon.

Disregarding the intense enemy small-arms, automatic-weapons, and mortar fire, he moved about the battlefield administering last rites to the dying and giving medical aid to the wounded. When an exploding mortar round inflicted painful multiple wounds to his arms and legs, and severed a portion of his right hand, he steadfastly refused all medical aid. Instead, he directed the corpsmen to help their wounded comrades and, with calm vigor, continued to move about the battlefield as he provided encouragement by voice and example to the valiant marines.

Upon encountering a wounded corpsman in the direct line of fire of an enemy machine gunner positioned approximately 15 yards away, Lt. Capodanno rushed a daring attempt to aid and assist the mortally wounded corpsman. At that instant, only inches from his goal, he was struck down by a burst of machinegun fire. By his heroic conduct on the battlefield, and his inspiring example, Lt. Capodanno upheld the finest traditions of the US Naval Service. He gallantly gave his life in the cause of freedom."

CHAPTER 4

BACK TO REAL LIFE

St. Philip, another of Christ's apostles, was crucified for the faith in 0061. He died for the Greater Glory of God.

I had two months to go in my enlistment when I got home, but the Marine Corps gave me a hardship discharge in December of 1967 so that I could work at a higher rate of pay, pay my parents' bills off and support my kid brother Ti-Bert.

My father recovered from his heart attack and by the fall of 1968 we were hunting together again. But the next summer he suffered a stroke that paralyzed his right side and his esophagus. He did not eat one bit of food or drink one drop of water from 1969 until 1982 when he passed away. It all went into him through a feeding tube, and he spent the rest of his life in a nursing home called Montello Manor.

After the Marine Corps, I went to work as a grocery clerk at Cottle's supermarket on Sabattus Street in Lewiston. I was free from commitment and frequently dated. At one point, a tall, slim girl who worked behind the fish counter caught my eye. She had long dark hair and hazel eyes with an independent glint to them.

Her name was Donna Nelson and she worked part-time with her mother, Pauline, who also tended the seafood counter. I had been told that she thought I was cocky and conceited and if I asked her for a date, she would most likely turn me down. Fortunately, at a company picnic in the summer of 1968, we were on the same relay race team, and we won handily. She was strong, good-looking, fast on her feet and full of fun and love. I decided that she would one day be my wife. She was the girl I had been looking for, the one I would take up Sabattus Mountain, the woman who would bear our children.

Donna came from a large family, the fifth child of eight. Her father, whose family established roots in Maine in the late 1800s, owned a small farm on the eastern outskirts of Lewiston where he raised chickens and cows for milk.

That summer, 1968, she was entering her senior year at Lewiston High School. I decided to give it a shot. My gut told me she wanted to date me. I asked her out and she said yes. I was ecstatic. The next day, on our first date, I took her up Sabattus Mountain. It was a hot day and a moderately difficult climb. We reached the top and gazed down at Sabattus Lake. We embraced, and I knew right then and there that my life was going to be fulfilled, and that Donna would stand by me no matter what.

(Our theme music in those years was "Angel in the Morning" by Juice Newton and "This Guy's in Love With You" by Eddie Ames.)

And she did. Thirty years later she would be subjected to intensive questioning by the FBI as they tried to sort out the reasons for my terrible psychological collapse. And just as I sensed at age 13, I suffered greatly. The worst pain was knowing that I brought so much agony to the love of my life. Nothing is more disturbing than having complete strangers probe into your life by asking your wife: "Did he ever abuse you?" "Did he ever abuse the kids?" "Has he ever violated national security?" "How much did he drink?" "Has he ever driven the Bureau car under the influence?" "Has he ever threatened you?" "Are you afraid of him?"

The inquisition was an ordeal for her and added to my mental anguish, setting back my recovery from the breakdown by several weeks. But Donna and I had no choice. My career and livelihood were on the line. We had to allow them to break the sacred trust of spousal privilege, which is available to all criminals, akin to the lawyer-client relationship. I had never given anyone any reason to ask most of those questions.

However, as I'll explain later, it *was* fair to ask about my drinking habits.

Back to January of 1969. I popped the question. I had the diamond ring in my pocket and Donna and I took a walk in a field behind her father's house, on Gayton Road about four miles from my neighborhood. We were crunching our way through the snow when we hit a pocket of drifted white stuff that was waist-deep. Donna got bogged down and asked me to help her. I said, "Sure, after you agree to marry me." Her eyes opened wide, I gave her a hand, and she hugged me and said she would.

Later that evening, after we announced our good news, Donna's father was burning trash in a 55-gallon drum outside the house. In those days it was legal to burn trash. Somehow a .22-caliber bullet had found its way into the trash. The heat of the fire set it off and it grazed my future father-in-law, Ralph "Bud" Nelson, in the forehead. He staggered into the house with blood dripping from his head and said, "See what Don did. He caused me to shoot myself." Once we realized it was just a scrape, we all sat back and laughed.

Donna and I were married on Aug. 30, 1969, at St. Peter and Paul's Church, with Father Bouvier officiating. We both took the sacred oath in front of God to love one another until death do us part. We have lived by this sacred, immutable oath continually for 39 years.

In 1969, taking advantage of the GI Bill, I resumed my collegiate career at the University of Maine in Orono, majoring in wildlife management. The degree would fit right into my love of hunting, fishing, camping and the outdoors, which Donna enjoyed sharing with me.

I had considered a law enforcement career, but at the time the height minimum for the State Police and most local police departments was 5'8". I topped out at 5'6". So I muddled through my studies. Donna worked in the seafood department at the Shop 'n Save supermarket in Brewer, a town near Orono where we lived.

I occasionally took time off to hunt for pheasants, ruffed grouse, woodcock and ducks with Lady Anne, my great little Springer spaniel. And I was eager to join the job market, particularly since Donna was pregnant and due about Feb. 1.

But it became apparent that there weren't many jobs in wildlife management, and that the few up for grabs were essentially political plums. One day, at the university's career center, I found an announcement about a Civil Service examination. One of the jobs available was with the Customs Service. There were no height restrictions. It was a law enforcement and regulatory agency, and relatively free of political influence.

I took the test and was delighted to find myself ranked at the top of the list in New England. In the early spring of 1972, the Customs Service invited me to join. My daughter Karen had been born right on time and I was seeking a career-type position to support the family. My starting job was as a customs inspector at the St. Aurelie Port of Entry

55 miles northeast of Jackman, Maine, which is about as remote as you can get. I was going to be a GS-5 inspector -- salary of $5,000 -- with a potential journeyman level of GS-9. The government would pay for housing and utilities. In September 1972, after I graduated with a BS in wildlife management, my federal career was underway.

Fundamentally, I was responsible for searches and seizures of contraband and undeclared items. For the undeclared items, we would charge a civil penalty equal to the value of the item, but that was always mitigated to a lower penalty absent any aggravating factors. I also collected duties and various other revenues.

By far most of the public I dealt with were Canadian woodcutters from the neighboring Quebec towns of St. Aurelie, St. Zacharie, St. Proper, St. Pamphille and other French Canadian villages.

Since I spoke French, I was an immediate hit with the woodcutters. I treated them with respect. When I seized items such as chain saw chains, chain saws, chain saw bars, skidder chains or skidder tires that they tried to smuggle into the United States, I explained the laws governing the seizures and accompanying fines that would be imposed.

The woodcutters were allowed to bring their own equipment in if they declared it to Customs and paid duty and applicable taxes on the goods. If they did not declare, the item was seized and a fine was imposed.

At St. Aurelie, I met some imposing people. The average woodcutter was strong and physically fit, starting to chop wood at the crack of dawn and going until 4 p.m. every day, generally four days a week, without complaint. They arrived in Maine between 4 a.m. and 7 a.m. on Mondays, drove to their respective camps and started cutting. At 3 p.m. every Thursday, they emerged from the woods and returned to their families in Canada.

In December 1972, I met Maine Game Warden Bill Downing, a rookie who started his career at St. Aurelie, and his wife Jeannie. They had a son named Greg and a daughter named Angela. The Downings and the Goulets were the only two families living on the American side of the border. Bill and I often met on the other side of the gate, in Canada, and enjoyed a few beers after work at Benoit Caron's bar, about 200 feet from the Customs House.

In 1992, midway through the active portion of the Francis Boots case, I needed a "safe house" for Fred Moore and myself. We were at the point where we had to transcribe 60-plus tapes of conversations recorded undercover between Fred, who was wearing a wire, and the Mohawks and their co-conspirators. We also wanted to let the heat die down and make sure that Fred had not been compromised.

Bill Downing, who lived about 30 miles from me in the Bar Harbor area, put me in touch with a game warden supervisor. That led to our stay for a week at a Maine warden camp on East Musquash Lake, off Route 6, near Danforth in the eastern part of the state northeast of Bangor. Bill and the warden supervisor were two of just four people who knew of our secret location. The other two were Supervisory Special Agent James Powers from the Boston Division and my special agent partner, whose name I cannot reveal, in our Bangor office.

Several years later, Bill came through for me again. In late February 1998, when mental disorders struck me down, I visited Bill to explain my dire circumstances just before I checked into Massachusetts General Hospital. He was a close and true friend and someone I turned to in my moment of need. I broke down in front of him, and he told me, "It's not your fault. They made you what you are." (I wanted to agree with him, but most of my suffering was related to post-traumatic stress disorder, as I found out later.)

Back in St. Aurelie in June 1973, our 16-month old daughter Karen had developed a serious chronic ear infection, which needed weekly attention. The closest ear doctor was in Waterville, Maine, 140 miles away from the St. Aurelie Port of Entry. I knew there were several customs inspector openings at Dorval Airport in Montreal. I applied and was transferred in December on a two-year appointment. Three weeks later, my son Keith was born on Christmas Day. And my daughter's health improved dramatically thanks to ear, nose and throat doctors in Montreal.

At the airport, we "pre-cleared" U.S.-bound airline passengers. I got involved in intercepting stolen fur coats destined for the New York market and seizing six pounds of marijuana. Amazingly enough, the man carrying the marijuana was a Nigerian passenger wielding a ceremonial sword. On another occasion, I found $20,000 of currency in a hollowed-out shaving cream can. I got suspicious when I hefted it in my hand and held it near my ear and shook it.

But what stood out for me was the search and identification of an Italian Mafioso from Sicily. Accompanied by a local hood, Guiseppe Napolitano, this Sicilian, whose name I don't recall, presented himself for inspection one night at 10:45 -- 15 minutes before his flight to New York City.

I recognized Guiseppe from previous encounters and knew that arrival for pre-clearance just minutes before departure time was a common ploy to rush the Customs and Immigrations inspection process. Upon presentation of the Sicilian's luggage, Guiseppe did all the talking as the Sicilian did not speak English. I carefully documented and committed to memory his name, destination and other items of useful intelligence. Guiseppe was not flying to New York City with this guy. He was merely there to facilitate his clearance.

After searching the luggage and entering his name into the Treasury Enforcement Computer System (TECS), I let them go their way. I called the U.S. immigration inspector on duty and briefed him, then followed the two until they parted company after Immigration cleared the Sicilian. Guiseppe went back to the main airport terminal and I watched the Sicilian board the Air Canada flight to New York, which had been delayed a couple minutes for him.

I returned to my post, closed down all the systems and went home. About 2:30 a.m. the phone rang. A federal Drug Enforcement Agency agent wanted to know about the Sicilian's boarding activities. They had been alerted that a Sicilian would enter the country to do a contract on a member of one of the New York crime families. I told him all I knew and went back to sleep, as I had to start work at 6 a.m. (We all worked 12- to 16-hour days thanks to a shortage of inspectors.)

What happened to the Sicilian after that, I don't know, but I know that the episode got me thinking about being a special agent with the Customs Service. Chasing bad guys was more appealing to me than the routine of checking luggage. Special agents investigated foreign criminal and local enterprises involved in smuggling. And in those days, before the Drug Enforcement Agency came along, Customs agents did drug interdiction and drug-running investigations.

I didn't get my wish because there were no openings for special agents in the Northeast. But the Montreal experience was still a fruitful one. Among the 35 inspectors I befriended on the pre-clearance beat in Montreal was Thomas "Burgie" Bourgoin, a combat Marine who had served in Vietnam. For the next 16 years, we were hunting partners, going after trophy whitetail bucks in rugged areas of northern Maine. Along with my brothers-in-law Randy and Skip Nelson, my nephew Dave Nelson and Al Borazelli, we spent days and weeks roaming ridges and mountains in areas with names like Black River, Glazier Brook Mountain, Fish Pond, Cold Stream Mountain, the Allagash, Second Musquacook Lake and Little Chase Stream Pond.

After my two-year assignment in Montreal ended, I was transferred back to the Jackman Port of Entry (POE). Jackman, on Route 201 in northwestern Maine, is the gateway to Quebec City. Donna and I had two children then, Karen and Keith. On June 23, 1976, Donna gave birth to Kristen.

I became familiar with the import and export of goods by rail and the clearance of small aircraft arriving from Canada at private airports, seized drugs and contraband on numerous occasions, and made several arrests.

When Donna could get away from the kids, we spent some of our free time at the Northland Hotel in Jackman. We'd have a few drinks and socialize with other inspectors and the locals. The popular songs back then were "New Kid in Town" and "Hotel California" by the Eagles.

In fact, The Northland became my personal watering hole. In the mid-'70s, Readers Digest reported that more beer was consumed in Jackman per capita than anywhere else in the United States. I was socializing with big, strong, independent men and women who worked hard all day cutting timber, laying railroad ties and manning shifts at the lumber mill.

One night, Robert Dutelli -- a local drinking hero who was as strong as a workhorse and highly respected and loved in town -- challenged me to a beer-drinking contest. OK, I figured, I can handle him. But after consuming 12 to 14 Buds in about four hours, I conceded to Robert, who had more than doubled my intake. (Some time later, Robert fell down the stairs at his home, broke his neck and died.).

The next day, I suffered at work. Although Donna and I shared some great times at the Northland, I witnessed the devastating effects of alcoholism on a few locals -- unemployment and deteriorating health. I really didn't want to be part of that.

At the time, I was also beginning to receive sexually related phone calls. When I arrived home from work, the phone would ring. I'd pick it up and at the other end was a female who would breathe lustily into the phone with major sexual overtones. She would also utter cries of ecstasy just as she hung up. It amounted to sexual harassment of a sort, I suppose.

Unfortunately, there was no caller ID in those days. We decided it was time to get out of Jackman, particularly since Donna and the kids preferred living in a bigger town. So I applied for an opening in the Calais, Maine Port of Entry and got the assignment.

In the fall of 1978, we moved to Calais, on the far eastern border with New Brunswick. I still yearned to be a Customs special agent, but there was only one agent, Bob Veal, in Maine and he was at the Houlton Port of Entry, well north of Calais. Bob tried several times to get me assigned as a special agent to help him out, but to no avail, even though my performance evaluations were among the highest in the region.

While in Calais, I forged strong ties with our Canadian counterparts and the Royal Canadian Mounted Police. We shared intelligence that resulted in several arrests and seizures of drugs, currency and other contraband. (It is illegal to import or export more than $10,000 in currency or negotiable instruments without filing a currency report with the U.S. Customs Service. The law making it illegal was passed in the 1970s primarily to deter drug smuggling and other forms of illegal activities such as loan sharking.)

My Canadian Customs contact was Guy Humphrey, a great law enforcement officer. My RCMP contact was Greg McAvoy, and my contact with the Calais police was Sgt. Ralph Bridges. (Later, as the Boots investigation got underway, I called Ralph and asked him what he knew about Fred Moore.)

By 1980, I was getting restless. The special agent position looked like a dead end. That fall, while working at the Mill Town crossing, I did a routine search of the trunk of a prominent Portland, Maine attorney. I discovered some pornography, a form of contraband, and seized it. The attorney was quite upset, and he wanted his stuff back. I let him make a phone call.

Thirteen years later, while on an FBI investigation, I learned that that phone call had gone to Assistant U.S. Attorney Bill Browder. Bill told me in 1993 that when he got that call, "I wouldn't touch it with a ten-foot pole." The Portland attorney was not charged.

CHAPTER 5

STREET AGENT

St. Matthias was the apostle chosen to replace Judas of Iscariot. He was beheaded in 0065. He died for the Greater Glory of God.

I was working at the Mill Town crossing one evening when I read an article about the new FBI director, William Webster. His progressive notions impressed me. Agents would be performing more undercover operations and working with relatively new statutes such as the Racketeering Influenced Corrupt Organization (RICO) law. I thought to myself, "Wow, that would be a great job, working as a special agent for the FBI."

I made some inquiries and learned that I would qualify for a position with the agency through their "modified program." I had always thought that you needed a degree in accounting or law to be considered for an appointment in the Bureau. But under the modified program, I needed a four-year college degree and three years of full-time work experience to qualify.

I met those criteria, so I contacted the FBI in Boston and asked for an application. I was 32 years old and in three more years I wouldn't qualify to apply for any federal law enforcement position, as the cut-off age was 35. I realized that if I got the job, I'd have to move the family several more times before the end of my federal career. Donna and I discussed it, and she gave me the go-ahead.

It took about two weeks to gather information for the application, and I submitted it to the Boston FBI office. A couple of months passed and I got word that I qualified to take the test. I took it and failed, but then they told me there'd been a computer glitch, so I took it again. The second time, in 1980, I passed, and they ranked me fifth out of some 2,100 applicants. I was pretty excited.

Meanwhile, Donna and I had begun to attend the Church of the Immaculate Conception in Calais. Donna was not yet a Catholic and I had allowed my faith to lapse for 15 years or so. I thought of Father Capodanno frequently when I returned to the church. His death had had a far greater effect on me than I was willing to admit.

After making a long confession, I began to receive Holy Communion. In 1981, Donna became a baptized Catholic, received her first Communion and was confirmed in the Church of our Lord in March 1982. Father Arseneault was our pastor.

Around September 1981, I was told that as soon as a class opened at the FBI Academy in Quantico, Virginia, I would be asked to join the ranks of special agents. Then I got word to show up for training at the end of February 1982. I left my position with the Customs Service on Feb. 20 and was sworn into the FBI in Boston on Feb. 22, without a break in federal service.

I had beaten the maximum law enforcement entry age of 35 by eight months and would be one of the old salts at the Academy. Two other special agents in our class were older than I. I said a temporary good-bye to Donna and the kids and flew from Bangor to Washington, D.C., where I met my classmates and got an initial briefing.

Then they put us on a bus for Quantico. I passed a physical fitness test, although my two-mile run time wasn't too great. Luckily, I passed the initial physical tests because about four weeks later, in a bad guy-vs.-two-good-guys takedown situation, I seriously injured and stretched the tendons in my right foot. Rather than send me home to recover and join another class later, the Bureau allowed me to stay with my class while I recovered.

The training at the Academy was fairly intense in the sense that you could only fail once on any given test. If you failed two tests -- whether the same one twice or two different tests -- you'd be asked to leave. We were tested on subjects such as constitutional law, forensics, case development, report writing and internal documentation -- teletypes, memos, informal reports called "inserts" and FD-302s, which are the results of interviews of individuals.

The firearms training was superb -- and a bit too realistic for me. One time, while I was standing at the FBI range firing line, some nearby drug enforcement agents popped an illumination round that whooshed up into the sky. I guess I was pretty nervous at the time because I fell to the ground immediately. Must have been a Vietnam flashback. I found my reaction pretty embarrassing.

At the time, the Academy had an open drinking policy. After hours, you could go to the Board Room, the Academy's watering hole, which was generally filled to capacity in the evenings. You could also have beer and liquor in your room. Like others, I consumed very little alcohol during the week -- a beer here, a beer there. But come Friday, we managed to have a very good time.

My best friends at the Academy were John Lewis and Sherry Farrar. Lewis and Farrar would both rise to near the top -- Farrar as an assistant director and Lewis as a deputy assistant director and special agent in charge of the Oklahoma City and Phoenix divisions.

John had an unusual sense of humor and always tried to set me up. One day, after I left my room to attend classes, he placed a plastic baggie containing a leafy substance under my bed, figuring the cleaning ladies would find it. John knew I was a stickler about illegal drugs.

Sure enough, about 9:30 a.m. that day, the unit chief, John Burke, came to the classroom, publicly announced that he wanted to see me in his office and left. When I got there, he dropped the bag on his desk and said the cleaning ladies had found marijuana under my bed.

I was absolutely dumbfounded. But then I looked closer and recognized it for what it was, oregano. So we had a good laugh, and then decided to set up John. I returned to the classroom, feeling the stares of my classmates. John, I noticed, had a huge smile on his face.

That's when I got him. Wearing a somber face, I walked to my desk, picked up my books and materials and said a general good-bye. I was done, and I walked out of the room, where Burke joined me. The class counselor went in and told my classmates that I had been kicked out of the Academy. Naturally, everyone was stunned, and John's expression turned very serious. Once they got the joke, I returned to the classroom and quietly went to my seat and sat down. I'd had the last word.

During 15 weeks at the Academy, I learned a great deal about investigative techniques, the attorney general's guidelines -- how to apply for a wire tap, how to avoid violating suspects' rights, etc. -- the Bureau mission and other matters. I consistently shot a low 90 in firearms training, did okay on the six-mile run, and graduated in June. My orders were to return to Boston for a six-month assignment, with a further posting to follow.

Back I went to Calais for a wonderful and joyous reunion with my family who were, and always have been, the center of my existence. Donna told me she had played Willie Nelson's song "You Were Always On My Mind" constantly while I was away.

We sold the house, hired a U-Haul and moved our household goods to Dracut, Mass., where we lived for six months. I reported to the Boston Division in June 1982. They assigned me to the Applicant/Civil Rights Squad, which did background investigations on presidential appointees and presidential pardons and enforced the Civil Rights Act.

While I was in Boston, my dad passed away. Although I'd been there only a couple weeks, Boston special agents and support people sent a beautiful flower arrangement to the funeral home, and Special Agent Charlie W., who had done my background investigation in the Lewiston area, took the time to attend the wake. That sort of concern touched my whole family. People in the FBI took care of each other. I never forgot that moment, even at the worst of times.

In the next few months, I did several civil rights investigations involving allegations of police brutality by local officers and investigations of presidential appointees. On one occasion, I got involved in foreign counterintelligence surveillance, although under Bureau rules I can't go into any details.

At every opportunity, I volunteered to help case agents assigned to other squads. Some time in late summer, about 3 p.m. or so on a Friday, a call came across the loudspeaker requesting volunteers to assist in an arrest, search and seizure in Chelsea, Mass. The subject was a member of a known armed bank robbery ring. Along with another agent I'll call "Gerry," I volunteered.

We arrived at the suspect's home and surrounded it with agents and local uniformed police officers. Gerry and I were assigned to perimeter security in front of the home. When the case agent knocked, announced and entered, the suspect fled through the back door, running all the way. He circled towards the front and sped by us. Gerry and I followed at a run, but I had unwisely chosen to wear my fancy brown cowboy boots, which weren't made for moving fast. Gerry took off in a different direction, trying to cut the guy off.

I ran around a street corner and saw that a big, burly Chelsea cop had nabbed the guy. He pushed the subject up against the wall of a building and said, "What the fuck do you think I am, a track star?" A very comical scene.

There were other events that stand out -- guarding $550,000 in currency that had been stolen in an armored car robbery by a guy nicknamed "Five by Five" while a slew of bank employees counted it by hand; and flying from Boston to Washington, D.C., with the partial remains (bone fragments) of a guard who had been brutally murdered at the John F. Kennedy Library complex for forensic analysis.

Near the end of the summer, I got orders to report to the Muncie, Ind., Resident Agency, a three-agent office, by the middle of December 1982. Under the Bureau transfer policy at the time, it was going to be a two- to four-year assignment. At home that evening, I told Donna that Muncie was in the middle of corn country, which meant good pheasant-hunting possibilities. She'd done some ruffed grouse hunting in Maine, and I figured she'd enjoy going after pheasants. I told her we'd buy a nice house and we'd be comfortable. Her only concern was being so far away from our beloved Maine.

Arriving in Muncie, I met the two senior agents I'd be working with, Roy Martin Mitchell and Howard (I don't have permission to use his full name). They were very helpful, but what I didn't like hearing was that there were no pheasants in Indiana as the soil lacked certain compounds that they needed to survive.

One of my early cases involved a high-priority DEA fugitive named Jeffrey Alan Doyle, who'd been indicted for involvement in a major cocaine distribution network in the Midwest. His hometown was Anderson, Ind., part of the Muncie Resident Agency territory.

I spent the next 15 months chasing him down. I can't go into many details here because the information is too sensitive and could jeopardize lives today. I *can* say that he was apprehended during a routine traffic stop in the Carolinas or Georgia. Thanks to that case, I met Lt. Ed Hanlon, who was in charge of the Vice, Intelligence and Narcotics (VIN) Division of the Anderson Police Department. Ed became a great friend and I consider him one of the true living heroes I have encountered.

When we met in early January of 1983 at police headquarters, he took me upstairs to meet some detectives. One was Gary Burke, a former Marine. Moments before our introduction, Burke came up behind me, slapped my right shoulder in a welcoming gesture, and ran his right hand down my right side, obviously to see if I was armed. I introduced myself and thought I'd better watch out for this guy.

Burke was a good friend of Police Officer Jack Vaughn, also a former Marine. I learned later that he was alleged to have been involved in several types of criminal activity, which he referred to as "taking care of business."

After Hanlon and I went back to his office, I told him about my interest in Jeff Doyle. He said he'd help in any way, but warned me to be careful about who I dealt with, meaning other cops. I told him I'd work only with he and his partners in the VIN unit, as well as Police Chief Frank Burroughs.

By February, Ed and I had established a productive working relationship, and he was ready to open up to me about some serious matters going on in his own backyard. One evening when I was at the police department, he said, "We've got to talk."

We went out to the parking lot and got into my Bureau car, a full-sized sedan. We sat and talked for three and a half to four hours. Ed spoke of a cancer in the police department, a cocaine conspiracy involving police officers and a local attorney, an illegal gambling enterprise, and allegations of extortion of prostitutes by certain members of the police department. He described a connection linking all these criminal activities. The central figure appeared to be the police officer, Jack Vaughn. Would I help? Absolutely.

The next day I opened a criminal case listing as subjects Jack Vaughn, attorney David O. Carmony, Calvin Cannon, the owner of the illegal gambling enterprise, and others. Ed warned me that Vaughn was a former Marine, strong as a bull, with an extremely volatile personality. And he was unpredictably dangerous.

During the next few weeks of the investigation, I got a telephone call from a cooperating witness who said that Carmony appeared to be planning a hit-for-hire scheme. He wanted to kill an unknown homosexual male somewhere north of Marion, Ind. The intended victim allegedly had a large cache of gold. Unfortunately, we were never able to identify him. The witness was willing to wear a wire to gather evidence.

I contacted the Indiana State Police and they joined our investigation. What we ended up with was a loose task force. Over the next several months, we made some great strides. Based on probable cause established by information from the cooperating witness, we obtained a federal search warrant for Carmony's office and his home.

We'd also been told that the attorney was hiding a big stash of cocaine. But as we were planning the search, we heard there was a leak and Carmony knew we were coming. Now we had to hurry. Fortunately, he hadn't quite cleaned out his office and home.

Eight or nine of us swooped into the building -- FBI agents, State Police detectives and Anderson cops. Our search didn't turn up much except for a silencer, which I discovered hidden in a closet. But that was enough for the U.S. attorney to charge Carmony with possession of a silencer (a federal offense) try him and convict him. As a result, he was disbarred and placed on five years of federal probation.

Thanks to information from the Indiana State Police, we also targeted a nationally known brothel just outside Anderson that was featured in Playboy magazine in the late 1970s. Many prominent individuals frequented the place, and it had been protected by corrupt local public officials, allowing uninterrupted service for some 30 years. I believe the name was The Indiana Motel.

We knew that when the local police busted the place in the past, the prostitutes were publicly identified only under their aliases. Apparently, that was part of the agreement they had with the local police. So the task force came up with a plan. We sent in an undercover State Police officer, and then used the real names of the prostitutes when he busted them. The scheme worked, and the prostitutes were furious.

Eventually, we developed witnesses who told us that Vaughn and others were on the take, getting "vig" to protect the prostitution ring. (Vig is underworld shorthand for receipt of any illegally obtained money, usually connected with gambling.) For the first time in decades, the place was shut down.

I approached the assistant U.S. attorney about charging Vaughn and others. He declined. Because the prostitutes hadn't paid income tax on their illegal earnings, the assistant U.S. attorney ruled that they were unreliable witnesses.

Late in the summer of 1983, I got a call at the office from Jack Vaughn. In aggressive tones, he said he heard that I had him under investigation and he wanted to talk to me about it right now. I told him that was impossible and hung up. In the meantime, another agent and I came up with a way to neutralize Vaughn.

My FBI partner at the time, Special Agent E.B., agreed to help me interview Vaughn in about a month's time. We would let Vaughn stew in his own juices until then and interview him on our terms, not his. By questioning him at the Anderson Police Department we figured it would have a chilling effect on other officers who might be involved. What's more, we thought the interview would send a strong signal of support to all the honest cops on the police force.

We picked a date for the interview when Vaughn was scheduled to be on duty in uniform. Hanlon told me he'd be wearing a bulletproof vest, just in case Vaughn blew his top.

Special Agent E.B. and I set up the interview room. I planned to sit across a desk from Vaughn, and E.B., who was a pretty big guy, would sit immediately to Vaughn's right, ready to intervene physically if need be. We asked the dispatcher to call Vaughn in from his street assignment.

Before long, he walked in and sat down. I told him right up front that he was under investigation, and we recited a litany of our suspicions -- drug distribution, money laundering of drug proceeds, extortion, possible arson and assault with a deadly weapon. Sweat began to form on his face and he turned a bright red.

As I recall, Vaughn didn't say a word. We confirmed that he was the subject of an FBI investigation, and the interview ended. Vaughn took sick leave, and then the Anderson Police Department fired him. And he made it clear that he didn't like me, telling one acquaintance that when I was a baby my mother must have dropped me on my head.

Later on, after my transfer to New York City, I heard that in the mid-1980s Vaughn was arrested, charged, convicted and sentenced to eight years in prison for distribution of cocaine.

For his part, Calvin Cannon was convicted of operating a gambling enterprise. Heavily fined, he lost everything he had earned over the previous decades and died a broken man.

One less stressful sidelight of resident agency work is conducting background investigations on prospective agents. In Muncie, I helped check out John Pistole. I met John and his wife at their home in Anderson, and liked them both. John eventually was named deputy director of the Bureau -- second in command below the director and the highest non-appointed FBI official. Just recently, Ed Hanlon told me that John Pistole was the most distinguished citizen ever to come out of Anderson.

Once I cut my teeth in Muncie working with informants and cooperating witnesses, investigating corruption, conducting fugitive investigations, doing drug and murder probes, using body wires, etc., I got my transfer orders. I was headed to New York City and I was due to start in May 1984.

Donna and I bid farewell to many close friends, particularly Dick and Sheila Bolduc and their children, who lived about six miles from us. Coincidentally, Dick and I had been members of Boy Scout Troop 118 in the late 1950s in Lewiston, Maine.

All along, I was sensitive to the effects that all transfers -- we'd been living a nomadic life since 1972 -- might have on Donna and the children. So far it looked good. They were all for their dad, and Donna was happy to go wherever I went. God was providing for us in every way.

But that didn't mean every move was easy. During our house-hunting trip to greater New York and southern Connecticut, the reality of moving from a low-cost-of- living area to a high one hit us pretty hard. Right away, Donna and I knew that we couldn't find affordable housing within a 100-mile radius of New York City.

Over the years, scores of newly transferred agents found themselves in the same predicament and many resigned because of it. In fact, it was a personnel crisis for the New York City office. Finally, the FBI got congressional authorization for a locality pay system. But in the meantime, Donna had to go to work as a nurse's aide, a natural because she is so kind and compassionate by nature.

In 1984, our youngest child was Kristen, 8. We went into temporary quarters, renting a summer home in Fairfield, Conn., while we looked for housing. Until I met other agents in New York City from the Fairfield area, commuting by rail and bus, a total of about 70 miles, meant leaving at 4:30 a.m. and getting home about 7:30 p.m. -- a long day and a melancholy prospect.

My first day on the job, I was assigned to Supervisory Special Agent A.G.'s squad, C-11 -- part of the Organized Crime/Drug Enforcement Task Force in New York City. After reporting in, I met the assistant special agent in charge, who told me, "Your reputation precedes you. But realize that here in New York you're a small fish in a big ocean. Put in your time here as comfortably as you can." Taken aback at first, I later saw it as a gentle warning that I would be in for the long run.

Then I met my new squad mates, including Rick Mosquera and Gary Voss. Voss told me he lived close to Fairfield, and he drove me home that night in a Bureau car. Instantly, my transportation concerns were alleviated. Not only did he take me to and from work every day, but Gary and I became close friends and worked together on three different squads during my time in New York.

The priority for C-11 was a major investigation into the New York City Chapter of the Hells Angel Motorcycle Club. The main targets of the probe were the president, Sandy Alexander, and the vice president, Charles "Chuck" Zito. With most of the club's members eventually implicated in a drug distribution conspiracy, the squad directed the lion's share of its efforts the next year at getting evidence for arrests and convictions.

And thanks to the courageous efforts of an FBI undercover agent, a substantial nationwide investigation into the Hells Angels, including the New York City club, was underway. The operation was called "Rough Rider."

The FBI developed enough probable cause to wire-tap certain phones, which allowed C-11 to listen in on Hells Angels calls for several months during the fall and winter of 1984-85.

At one point toward the end of the investigation, I served a federal grand jury subpoena on Joel "Big Joe" Kaplan, a close associate of the Hells Angels who owned and operated a tattoo parlor in a middle-income neighborhood in Yonkers, N.Y. I made the trip by myself, but I should have taken someone with me.

As soon as I entered the tattoo parlor, I was instantly "made" by the friends and clients of Joel. After all, I was wearing a three-piece suit. Immediately, I was surrounded by six thugs who got quite verbally forceful: "Who the fuck are you? What the fuck you doin' here? What the fuck do you want with Joe anyway?" Somehow I managed to maintain my composure, serve the subpoena and leave.

Before we attempted to take the Hells Angels down in the spring of 1985, the squad supervisor asked me to develop a security plan for the agents and police officers who would make the arrests and subsequent searches in and around New York City. Reviewing old Hells Angels cases and intelligence, I came up with a security paper and briefed scores of agents and law enforcement officials on potential threats. Over 500 agents and law enforcement officers would participate in the operation.

As the time to act neared, the supervisor assigned me to coordinate the agents -- about 12 of them -- who would make the arrests at Zito's place and the tattoo parlor. We were after Chuck Zito and Joel Kaplan. I had studied both of them pretty well. Zito was well connected with prominent actors, actresses, show host celebrities and other famous people. I also knew of his reputation for violence against anyone who crossed him.

Working with the FBI office in New Rochelle, where Zito lived, we drew up a plan -- simultaneous early-morning arrests and searches at the Zito residence and the tattoo parlor. It was all part of Operation Rough Rider, a nationwide plan. I don't recall all the details, but the Hells Angels were also targeted in Bridgeport, Conn., upstate New York (Binghamton), Texas and New Mexico.

On the big day, I awoke at 2 a.m. and headed to the New Rochelle office, hoping that no one in the city -- that is, New York City, in New Jersey (where One-Armed Bert, a Hells Angel who had lost an arm making a homemade bomb, lived), in New Rochelle, or elsewhere -- would be hurt. By chance, I heard the song, "The Day Chicago Died" on the radio on my way to work.

I hooked up with the Zito team and went to the moderate-income neighborhood where he lived. Several of us had watched his house occasionally over the previous three months.

We knocked and announced ourselves, but to our dismay, Zito wasn't home. Apparently he and "One-Armed Bert" had gone to the West Coast. Eventually, we learned that Zito and One-Armed Bert had visited with a prominent actor in California and boarded a plane for Japan to render judgment on a Japanese motorcycle gang in Tokyo that had "struck for" (applied for) Hells Angels colors. The front office quickly contacted Japanese law enforcement authorities, who arrested them shortly after they got off the plane. They spent several months in a Japanese jail awaiting extradition.

Leaving Zito's, we went to Big Joe's, where we found him in handcuffs. About that time, we heard that there had been a shoot-out in Bridgeport involving a Hells Angels member or associate. He apparently had shot a state trooper in the stomach when the trooper and FBI agents tried to enter his home on a search.

As it turned out, Zito got six years in prison for his role in distributing narcotics. I don't know what became of Joel Kaplan. I think Sandy Alexander, the chapter president, got 15 years.

A month or two after the Hells Angels takedown, in the summer of 1985, I located my old Marine Corps buddy Jim Hamfeldt in New Jersey. We got together and chewed over old times, and that renewal of friendship lasts to this day. In fact, during my time of anguish and despair, I often turned to Jim for guidance and compassion.

About the same time, Special Agent Voss left C-11 for Squad SO-2 (Special Operations – Group 2) at a location that I cannot mention for security reasons. It was, fortunately, considerably closer to where we lived. The squad's job was surveillance. Gary put in a word for me and in the fall of 1985 I transferred to join him. Along the way, Special Agent James Kallstrom, another combat Marine from Vietnam, encouraged me to join the squad. He was the chief of special operations for the FBI in New York City.

Meanwhile, we had bought a house on two acres in Seymour, Conn., with a large in-ground pool. Donna and I spent many evenings poolside during the warmer months, sharing a few drinks and talking about our future. Gary, his wife and kids often visited on weekends. My family attended Mass religiously. Life was good.

SO-2 conducted hundreds of surveillances and took thousands of photos of organized crime figures, Colombian cocaine drug dealers and money launderers, restaurant inspectors who took bribes, and several other suspected criminals. When I reported to SO-2, I was assigned the oldest car in the car pool. A year later when new cars came in, I was assigned a 1986 gray Mercury Capri that featured spoilers, a full police package and a speedy five-liter engine. I "lived" in that car for the next two years and thoroughly enjoyed it.

The most notable surveillance target we worked was a cold-blooded killer named Tommy "Karate" Pitera. Pitera was a "made guy" in the Bonanno crime family. In the early 1990s, thanks in part to our surveillance, he was convicted of six murders and suspected of at least

10 more. Articles I've checked out on the Internet show that Pitera may have been responsible for up to 30 murders.

Working with Special Agents Voss, J.M. and Ronnie "Baby" Norman, I was assigned to two different teams during the Pitera surveillances. So for 12-plus months, more than five percent of my Bureau career, all I did on the job was follow Tommy.

We kept track of him in teams, each consisting of six agents. Our daily routine usually started at his apartment in South Brooklyn and sometimes at his bar, Tommy's Place, also in South Brooklyn. When he was up to no good, such as collecting illegal proceeds, he "cleaned" himself before he began his rounds. For instance, he would drive down a one-way street, turn around at the end of the street and crawl out of there slowly to catch any agent following him by surprise.

Once he made you, he would leave the area, speed up, make multiple "back-ups" and sometimes stop, leave his car and stand on the sidewalk watching for surveillance. He caught me like that once. As I drove by, he smiled and picked up his right hand ever so slightly.

We didn't watch him 24 hours a day, but we averaged about 16. I'm sure he knew when we weren't watching him. In one recorded conversation, Pitera said that if he made any federal agents following him, he would engage them in a shootout. He had many weapons, including automatics.

Tommy was married once and his wife overdosed on drugs and died. That experience made local drug dealers his targets for torture and murder. He killed a few and dismembered them, stuffing the body parts in a suitcase. The next step, according to informants and cooperating witnesses, was to drive to the bird sanctuary on Staten Island and bury the suitcases.

At one point, FBI management approached me with a concern. Tommy and I were the same basic height and weight, and we resembled each other slightly. He usually wore a leather jacket and jeans during cold weather, as I did. The Bureau worried that if another mob family decided to hit Pitera, they might get me by mistake. I told management that I would take precautions accordingly, which meant being more vigilant and avoiding the areas where Tommy frequently had meetings. I also kept my distance and tried not to tail him too closely on foot.

Eventually, Tommy was convicted of six murders and sentenced to life in prison without parole. The big songs at the time were Billy Joel's "Keeping the Faith" and Bruce Springstein's "Born in the USA."

While doing surveillance of another mobster, Anthony Spero, I took some pretty revealing photographs in 1987 or 1988. I shot a picture of several mob-connected individuals talking to each other outside a store. They then left in their cars, apparently to commit a murder, as I found out much later.

In the year 2000, when I was still an agent, I was asked to testify about those photos in U.S. District Court in the Eastern District of New York. That posed a problem because in 1998 I suffered a psychological breakdown and was somewhat alcohol-dependent. When the Boston Division of the FBI heard that I might testify, they decided I would have to make my problems known to the U.S. Attorney's Office, which in turn would have to inform the defense attorneys.

Even though no disciplinary action had been taken against me, I still had to bring the issue to the U.S. attorney's attention. During the trial, it never came up. But there's a lesson in that for all law enforcement officers: You may want confidentiality about any treatment you're getting for mental illness or alcohol dependency, but during trial testimony, you'll have to give it up.

At the end of 1988, a new squad, SO-15, was forming. It would do court-ordered surreptitious entries into clubs, businesses, cars and residences, generally associated with mob activity. The squad would be composed of technically trained agents in various fields, and they needed street agents like me to provide security. It looked good, so I joined.

My first assignment with SO-15 was to accompany J.M. to the Ravenite Social Club in Lower Manhattan where the famous mobster John Gotti held court. J.M. and I were to provide security for the entry team, made up of Dave Swanson and Ken Doyle. It was a great feeling knowing that we finally had a hole card to play against "the Dapper Don."

It was about 2:30 a.m. and the job took maybe 45 minutes. J.M. and I kept a low profile while we guarded the front door of the apartment building next to the Ravenite and we encountered no trouble. That break-in and installation of a wiretap proved to be the move that put Gotti in jail for good because the wiretap caught him speaking with his attorney about his involvement in several murders and other crimes.

That kind of surveillance brought many cases to a successful conclusion. There's nothing harder to defend than your own voice captured on tape while you're plotting mayhem, murder or other criminal acts. I was deeply honored to be chosen to participate on this squad.

Supervisory Special Agent Ken Doyle headed the squad, and he and his primary relief supervisor, Drew Roberto, coordinated the entries. Both were great guys and knew their business thoroughly.

Membership in SO-15 allowed me to work with Special Agents Ken Reeder, Swanson and another agent, Ronnie "Baby" Norman, whom I hold in the highest esteem. They were the point men, repeatedly exposing themselves to danger and potential political embarrassment for the Bureau should they be caught. Over three years, we did several dozen entries. For instance, Gary Voss and I entered a social club in Queens at least six times to adjust cameras and electronic bugs.

At the time I was working with SO-15, my children began to worry about me and my job. After they went to bed about 9:30 every night, I headed down to the city to do surveillance. Then they got up at 7 a.m. and I stayed home all day long into the evening. Seeing me at home so much, they'd ask if I'd been fired. Eventually, they got used to it.

All three were doing great in high school. Keith was an outstanding football player, going both ways as defensive end and tight end. Both my daughters were cheerleaders, and the oldest one fell in love and eventually married her high school sweetheart. The prominent high school song of the time was Meatloaf's "Bat out of Hell."

In June or July of 1990, I heard about an opening in the Bangor, Maine Resident Agency. That looked pretty good because the New York commute was getting to me -- 95 miles one way. Some agents lived as far away as 120 miles. We simply couldn't afford housing closer to New York on our salaries. What's more, Donna and I wanted to get home to lay down some roots. I had enjoyed a truly satisfying career, but now it was time to get out from under 12-to-16-hour days, go back home and help out our native Mainers.

A remote location, the Bangor office covered 1,900 square miles and a population base of about 300,000. A check on the Office of Preference (OP) list showed that I was about 24th in line for a transfer to the Boston Division, which covered Bangor. It looked like I'd have to work another five to seven years in New York City before I could get what I wanted. I wondered how many agents with OP seniority over me would choose Bangor rather than Boston. So I called the agents ahead of me, and not one wanted to go to Bangor.

That evening, I went home and had a sit-down with the whole family. Donna and I had agreed that if one of the kids objected, we wouldn't go any further. Karen, our eldest, had graduated from high school. Keith was entering his senior year and Kristen was about to be a freshman.

Amazingly, not one of the kids objected to the career move. Sure enough, I was offered and accepted the Bangor job in the late summer of 1991. I joined Special Agent J.S., who had conducted my northern Maine background investigation in 1981. I was to report in November 1991. I told my son that I'd find a way to keep him in Connecticut until he graduated from high school. His answer: "No, I want to be with my little sister."

SO-15 held a going away party for me. Everyone had a few beers and "Al the Carpenter," a good finish carpenter who worked at our office for the Bureau, put on a fabulous lunch. When I gave my little speech, several of the guys had tears in their eyes. We had been as close as Third Squad, Mike Company, Third Battalion, Fifth Marines, in Vietnam. However, it was time to move on.

On Nov. 16, Donna and I and several friends attended a dinner at a Mexican restaurant. The next day, I departed for Bangor, while Donna and the kids stayed in Seymour. They would join me after football season.

I arrived in Bangor on Nov. 18. Getting acquainted with J.S., I learned that federal statutes governing crimes on Indian reservations did not apply to the Native American population in northern Maine. As it turned out, the Maine Indian Land Claims Settlement Act had given the state the responsibility to investigate crimes on reservations. What's more, the larger tribes had their own police departments under the auspices of Maine law enforcement regulations.

Not long after I arrived at Bangor, I got a call that a staff sergeant with the U.S. Air Force had been shot in the back while he was sleeping at his home on Loring Air Force Base in Limestone, Maine. The sergeant was paralyzed. J.S. asked me to cover it because it looked like his wife shot him and she was a civilian, which put it under FBI jurisdiction. Her name was Dawn Dupuis.

Air Force investigators told me she wanted to leave the state that evening, so I had to get there in a hurry. I drove four hours to meet the investigators. As she tried to leave the base, Air Force personnel asked her to talk to the FBI, and she agreed. Shortly after I introduced myself to her, she confessed to shooting her husband in the back a few days earlier. She signed and initialed a statement to that effect. Further investigation showed that she had purchased .22 caliber rounds four days before the shooting.

After the confession, I contacted Assistant U.S. Attorney Jim McCarthy in Bangor, who authorized me to arrest her. Eventually the case was transferred to Assistant U.S. Attorney Tim Wing, who took it to trial in March 1992. To my amazement, the jury found her not guilty and she was freed.

I heard that a male juror who dominated the deliberations had made up his mind that she was not guilty. Eventually, his opinion ruled. We did have a full confession, we proved she was leaving the state for Nevada the night she was arrested, and we proved she had purchased the rounds for the gun four days earlier.

J.S. told me later that the U.S. Attorney's Office blamed me for the verdict. Consequently, Wing and I had quite a strained relationship after that. I suppose he had to blame someone for the failure, so why not me?

Three or four weeks after the verdict, I met Passamaquoddy Tribe Police Chief Fred Moore and that changed everything. A new substantive case is what I needed to prove myself to the U.S. Attorney's Office.

CHAPTER 6

EARLY LIFE ON THE PASSAMAQUODDY INDIAN RESERVATION AND BRIEF HISTORY AND CULTURE

As written by Frederick J. Moore III

St. Andrew, the brother of St. Peter, was scourged to death and preached for two days while dying in 0061. He died for the Greater Glory of God.

The Passamaquoddy Tribe has 2,000 to 2,200 members with some 750 at the Pleasant Point Reservation and another 1,300 to 1,400 at the Indian Township Reservation. As Pleasant Point police chief, Fred Moore dealt with all crimes covered by Maine criminal statutes, except murder. He investigated burglaries, robberies, assaults and other criminal matters. He attended the Maine Criminal Justice Academy, where he was asked by the instructors to sing the song "Running Bear."

Born at Pleasant Point in 1960, Fred provided these insights into his early life and some history of the tribe:

As a child of approximately 11 years of age, I remember waking to the sound of glass crackling, popping as if breaking under some kind of steady pressure. Lying on the couch looking up at tongue-like flames tipped in black as the smoke followed the flames. Smoke filling the room from the ceiling down to a few feet off the floor. Flames reaching like fingers across the ceiling and down the wall, thinning out as they reached ahead, rushing back to their source then coming forward again like waves reaching farther each time.

When the tips of the flames reached the top of the couch I realized that I couldn't get up; the heat was too intense. So I rolled off the couch and crawled toward the door on my hands and knees. It was not until I got out onto the door step that I realized people were standing around the yard -- many looking, some crying, some yelling to me to get out. It dawned on me that I was standing in my underwear, and people were watching me.

Turning back into the living room and laying on my back with the smoke about a foot or two above me, I managed to find my pants, and slid into them. Not having enough time to find my socks, I settled for my shoes and took them and crawled out of the house on my back. One time I attempted to get up but the heat was in the smoke and the combination of both would be enough to knock a grown person down.

Where's mumma? Where's dad? Men yelling around the corner, kids crying. I could hear my father making sounds I had never before heard. A couple of men holding him back from climbing a ladder. He was trying to climb into a bedroom through a window. It was his and mom's room, and that's where the baby stayed. She was around three months old.

Mom had gotten almost everyone out of the house, and went back in to get the baby. Overcome by smoke, she never made it out. But

I could swear I heard her say, "Get up! Get out!" as she went by the living room to get to the back room. My mother is still in the house. Did someone call the fire department? Some people just stared at me. Others ran past me to try to help. I jumped over the electric wire which melted off the house and was now sparking at its end, more crackling sounds, only this time a little sharper with a different smell.

Walking over to the phone booth about 50 yards away, picking up the phone and dialing "O" and asking if she could please send the fire truck. Running over to the neighbor's house across the street, asking if they could call the fire truck. The neighbor told me to stay right there. I wanted to find out what was going on as I watched my house go up in flames and eventually disappear. I asked those around if my mother would come out, did she get out, where did she go? No, they said she won't come out, she went in to get your sister and won't come out now.

She went to be with God. What about my sister? How come everyone is crying? The fire truck didn't come. I called them lots of times. Many more people running toward what was now a pile of burning debris -- our home just a few minutes earlier. Surreal, and almost unbearably sad. There were many of us children looking at each other and dad as he struggled with knowing he could not save my mother and sister, having struggled with his friends in an attempt to insert himself into peril as if to try and trade places with her. The fire truck never came. How come the fire truck never came? I called them from the phone booth. The operator said they were on their way, but they never came.

Then it was a beautiful day, a pleasant warm May morning. The green grass was already starting to show up and birds were out. All I could think to say was that my mother was still inside, until I saw law enforcement officials bringing out what looked like a bed on wheels with a blanket covering what looked like the shape of a person. The men doing it were very sad.

Although I did not understand what was going on, it was clear that my mother and sister would not be coming out, and that it was them on the bed with wheels covered with a gray blanket. My uncle Jim came over to help gather up the kids to be taken over to Grandmother's house. We were looking at the doghouse when I told Uncle Jim that I would have to sleep in the dog's house, but at least it's warm out. He said no you won't have to; you can stay at the house with us.

It was becoming clear that everything my life consisted of was now gone. I don't even have any socks or a jacket; now I have to live by myself.

Preparing to live a life consisted mostly of just getting by. I had to immediately develop a sense of independence in order to avoid situations of disappointment. Right away, it became obvious that I would be much better off if I went through life requiring little of others and expecting even less.

To simply get up in the morning and not have to scramble around on all fours in order to survive was surely a gift. Or was it? An experience like that can cause an impressionable young mind to consider all kinds of wild notions. Perhaps the most profound was the enduring question of purpose, one which would pursue this young person for the rest of his life: Why did I survive the fire?

The priest did not seem to have the answers. Nor did the nuns belonging to the Sisters of Mercy. Many times I would hear them telling others what happened in the tragedy. Why, I would ask, did God take my mother and sister? They would tell me that it was the will of God, and that he called Jeanette and my baby sister Gail to be by his side. But why? She was only three months old. What would God want to do that to us for? From this point in my life there would always be two sides to every story, and it would be up to me to decide which side I would believe.

The question of purpose would come up in my mind, over and over, with nearly every noteworthy experience. I would forever seek the true meaning of all things seen and heard, always questioning the true purpose in everyone and everything. In the years that followed, the question of purpose would translate to the pursuit of truth.

Strange white men showing up at the house, speaking English and acting very friendly, yet careful. These men are here to help us, my father was told. These people looked different. They were from away. The man from away with glasses wanted to know many things from my father, who was glad to tell the men anything they wanted to know. First we have to eat, he would tell them. "We're having chopped meat sandwiches and government cheese." The label read: "USDA NOT TO BE SOLD OR EXCHANGED" on every box, bag and can of food delivered to the reservation once a month.

Families would gather around the reservation school on delivery day to receive their rations of food. Some carrying burlap bags on their backs and others using wagons, wheelbarrows and a few vehicles. Nearly every family would be represented by someone seeking the usual allotment of food. Children would gather around to watch the excitement and try to get a package of raisins or prunes, maybe even a can of grapefruit juice. The government-supplied food became a staple for many families and the primary source of food for many individuals.

April 1991, Lafayette, Louisiana. The first Bureau of Indian Affairs Eastern Region Law Enforcement Conference -- the first annual conference of Indian police chiefs of the eastern United States. It was hosted by the

Division of Law Enforcement Services, Bureau of Indian Affairs. The conferences were designed to strengthen ties between Native American police departments and the numerous government agencies charged with enforcing federal statutes applicable to Indian country. The FBI described to the Indian police chiefs a long list of services available, mostly identification of offenders through a national crime information service and policies and procedures for getting help from the FBI.

Jim Duncan, Special Agent in Charge for the Inspector General at the Department of Interior (DOI), described how his department had established strong connections with Indian police: "You take up in the state of Maine, we have an excellent working relationship with the boys up on the two Passamaquoddy reservations."

That caught the attention of Passamaquoddy Tribe Indian Township Reservation Police Chief Alex Nicholas, who immediately shot a hard glance in my direction as if to say, What the hell is this? Chief Nicholas raised his hand to ask Duncan what exactly he had going on up in Maine, adding that he was from one of the Passamaquoddy reservations and knew nothing about this alleged relationship.

As Nicholas continued to glare at me as though I were hiding something from him, Duncan recognized his mistake and suggested that Chief Moore may wish to come up and help describe how these relationships are cultivated and strengthened. I approached Duncan, and he came close enough to tell me in a low voice, "Sorry about that, Fred. Looks like I screwed up. I had no idea this guy was here." Oh well, Jim, I told him, let's see what happens.

Knowing full well that there were several criminal investigations being conducted by the Inspector General's Office in Maine and specifically on the Indian Township and Pleasant Point Reservations, where I, Fred Moore, was police chief, Duncan would not elaborate. Instead he let me try to get around the issue.

Referring to a recently completed investigation, I gave an accounting of the work that had been done jointly. Nicholas must have seen it as a feeble attempt to hide something from him. He persisted and wanted to know if there was something going on in his community he didn't know about. Duncan came back to life and tried to lie to a room full of Indian police chiefs and their subordinates.

Finally it was time to take a break. Duncan walked up to me and said, "Hey Fred, is that the guy in Newell's pocket?"

"Yeah, he sure is!" I said. "This is going to get a little messy because he's going to go running right back to Newell."

Bob Newell was tribal chief of the Indian Township Reservation (also Passamaquoddy) and the subject of a major fraud investigation by the DOI Office of Inspector General, assisted by the Pleasant Point Reservation Police Department. Due to the control Newell exerted over his police chief, Interior's IG could not fully trust Nicholas to maintain confidentiality. The IG was sure that Nicholas would keep his tribal chief posted on any federal law enforcement activities targeting him or others with him.

Nicholas was not a target in any investigation by the Interior IG. The probe at that time was into allegations of fraud relating to construction of a tribal recreation center. The contractor on that project happened to be the brother of Cliv Dore, then the Pleasant Point tribal governor. The Dore brothers and Newell were implicated in fraudulent billing and over-charging and/or false statements on invoices, based on allegations by several tribal officials and individuals. No charges were ever filed.

Police Chief Nicholas was believed to be firmly in the pocket of Newell and therefore could not be trusted. Thus what I call the "axis of greed" -- Governors Newell and Dore along with Tom Tureen, one of the tribe's attorneys -- began to emerge.

That's how the first and what turned out to be the last chiefs conference of the Eastern Area Division began. After the break, the police chiefs identified major issues confronting the departments in their respective areas of operation.

August 1965. Cars parked along the road on both sides from the area of the church to the main highway, seeming like hundreds of vehicles and many hundreds of people. Off in the distance the sound of drums, people whooping, hollering and chanting Passamaquoddy tribal songs, echoing throughout the reservation over a loudspeaker.

They were Passamaquoddy tribal ceremonial days, founded by Mary Moore and based on teachings handed down through generations of tribal elders. Mary was taught the ceremonies and accompanying dances by her grandmother, Susan Neptune (my great-great-grandmother), who died in 1938 at the age of 107. She was a true tribal elder if ever there was one, a direct descendant of Francis Joseph Neptune, Hereditary Chief of the Passamaquoddy and leader of the Indians who fought in the American Revolutionary War.

It was Chief Neptune who fired the first shot during the Battle of the Rim at Machias, Maine, in August 1777. Asking the commanding officer for permission to fire the first gun, Chief Neptune said, "Watch the man on the bow of the ship." The colonel said it was an impossible distance, but told him to go ahead. A single shot rang out through the river basin.

The ship's captain was struck as he viewed the river from the bow of the British warship. He fell dead, leaving the crew and remainder of the force in disarray. Seeing the result from the river bank, the rest of the Native American fighters began yelling fiercely in tribal tongues as they fired volley after volley. That led to a quick surrender, thus ending one of the earliest and shortest battles of the American Revolution.

The Passamaquoddy took the side of the American colonies during the struggle against British rule. Ironically, the Passamaquoddy, who made up most of the fighting force, were the last to join in the struggle. Once in, the tribe guarded the coast from Passamaquoddy Bay to Castine on Penobscot Bay.

Passamaquoddy Indians are experts at handling canoes even in the roughest seas, and were instrumental in maneuvering revolutionary intelligence operatives in and out of enemy-occupied areas, mostly under cover of night or blinding fog. They moved officers by canoe through treacherous passages between islands and intertidal waterways, and at times commandeered enemy warships and sailed them into the hands of the American Navy.

The American revolutionary forces sought Passamaquoddy support because the tribe represented the balance of power in the region and served as a buffer between the warring factions in what is now eastern Maine. Writing to the Passamaquoddy on Christmas Eve 1776 before crossing the Delaware, General Washington asked the tribe to come to the aid of the colonies. By agreeing to help, the tribe ensured that the boundary between the U.S. and Canada was on Passamaquoddy Bay and not Penobscot Bay or Casco Bay, both of which are much further to the southwest.

Those are some of the stories told by tribal elders and handed down from one generation to the next. In this manner, the history and culture of the Passamaquoddy has been preserved for thousands of years. Their stories go so far as to describe ice giants (glaciers) moving from the north, crushing everything in their path until the land was destroyed.

August 1978. The Beltway, Washington D.C. We were walking along the interstate highway toward the Capitol, nearly 5,000 thousand Native

Americans from around the U.S. The plan called for the group to camp in Greenbelt Park and prepare for a rally in front of the J. Edgar Hoover Building (FBI headquarters) the next day. Another rally was scheduled for Malcolm X Park

It was a long day and the final leg of the journey known as the "longest walk," which originated in California earlier that year. The Passamaquoddy delegation joined somewhere around three days march from the Capitol. The purpose of the longest walk was to bring attention to treaty rights and the mistreatment of Native Americans by the government over the past 200 years.

It was the largest gathering of Native Americans I had ever seen in my life, with every known tribe in North America represented by a delegation of one form or another, from newborn babies to the eldest members of their respective tribes. Those of us from the Passamaquoddy sought out neighboring tribes with whom we had the most recent interaction -- the Iroquois Confederacy, including Mohawk and Onondaga Nations.

Campfires blazed every few hundred feet throughout the park. Children ran around playing, elders sat around talking, and groups of men and women sang tribal songs. You only had to walk a few hundred yards to see that the tribal encampments were situated much like the configurations of tribal or linguistic groupings throughout North America. The Algonquin were to the north and east, with the Iroquois to the west of us, and the Dakotas were beyond the Ojibwa or Chippewa and on and on.

After meeting up with friends and a visit to the Mohawk camp, my best friend Reggie Stanley and I ventured to the Camp of a confederation of western tribes to participate in a multi-tribal sweat lodge ceremony. Conducting the ceremony was a spiritual leader from one of the Dakota tribes.

It was the first time I had ever experienced the sweat lodge, and it was one of the most impressive ceremonies that I had experienced outside my own tribe. It wasn't so much the privilege of participating in a sweat lodge with so many prominent Native American leaders, or the fact that I could pray in my own language and be understood by tribal members from places like California and the Dakotas, where our language or anything closely resembling it is not spoken at all. (The ability of one native person to understand the language of another without having heard it spoken before has often been referred to as an "Indian thing." Beyond that, I can't explain it.)

It was the irony associated with the fact that my first and perhaps most moving experience with traditional ceremonies took place in Washington, D.C., of all places, in the midst of thousands of Native Americans from hundreds of tribes. Represented by dozens of prominent Native spiritual and political leaders from around North America. For a young man of 18 years who grew up on a reservation -- taught by nuns from early childhood that the ways of old have all gone away and the "Indians don't believe in that anymore" -- it was an awakening of the spirit. To feel that it was not only permissible to pray in one's own language, to the creator as seen in the eyes of Native Americans, but that it was also appropriate.

CHAPTER 7

GOING OPERATIONAL

St. James the Less, smaller than his brother St. James the Greater, was thrown from the Temple and clubbed to death for his Christian beliefs in 0062. He was another of Christ's apostles. He died for the Greater Glory of God.

The Six Nations make up the Iroquois Confederacy (Haudonausee)--Cayugas, Oneidas, Onondagas, Mohawks, Senecas and Tuscoraras. Collectively, they are the People of the Long House. The Mohawks have been regarded historically as the fiercest fighters of the six. The Mohawk Nation is on a reservation near Messina, N.Y., and Cornwall, Ontario. On the U.S. side, the Mohawks also occupy a piece of land known as St. Regis.

The Mohawks are also called "The People of the Flint" and are politically divided into traditional Mohawks and the Mohawk Warrior Society. The Mohawk Warrior Society has been involved in smuggling cigarettes and tobacco, narcotics (including cocaine) and guns into Canada, and general mayhem. In 1992, when we started the undercover operation and began to collect evidence, the leader of the Mohawk Warrior Society was Francis Boots, known as the War Chief. That meant that any militant violent activity would happen under his direction. In 1990, the Mohawk Warrior Society was known to have a massive weapons cache, which included automatic weapons and machine guns.

In the spring of 1990, a major gun battle took place between the traditional Mohawks and the Mohawk Warrior Society on the Akwesasne Indian Reservation in New York. It was a fight over gambling and illegal tobacco smuggling, both of which the traditional Mohawks opposed. Once Fred Moore told me in April 1992 that there would be tobacco smuggling, I opened a "case matter" (a file on a potential criminal investigation).

I also obtained a videotape from an FBI agent in Albany, New York, depicting the battle for Akwesasne. What I witnessed on that videotape was almost beyond belief. The Mohawk Warrior Society had the traditional Mohawks on the Akwesasne under siege, and gunfire erupted that was reminiscent of many of the battles I had fought in Vietnam. Two traditional Mohawks lay dead after the encounter.

Also on the video was a battle in the Oka Territory. Oka is a town in Quebec and part of the land in that town is owned by Native Americans of the Iroquois Confederacy of Quebec. That battle, in the late summer of 1990, involved a dispute over land and building a golf course, which the traditional Mohawk people supported and the Mohawk Warrior Society opposed. The ensuing firefight on the video was mind-boggling. It looked like thousands of rounds were fired and in the end, a Surete du Quebec police officer, Corporal Marcel LeMay, lay dead after having been shot in the mouth.

Both shooting incidents revealed the extreme firepower in the hands of the Mohawk Warrior Society and other Mohawk sympathizers and associates. Here again, the Oka firefight was reminiscent of combat conditions I had encountered in Vietnam.

As a result of those incidents and an effort by the RCMP to shut down the northern New York border to tobacco smuggling, narcotics smuggling and gun running, the Warrior Society looked for an alternative smuggling route. That's where the Passamaquoddy Tribe entered the picture. In April of 1992, Anthony Stanley, a Passamaquoddy, was contacted by a woman named Beverly Pierro, who represented Francis Boots, to open a smuggling route across the Maine-New Brunswick border to supply the Maritime Provinces with illegal tobacco.

Law enforcement thinking was that if an illegal tobacco route was established on that route, it would just be a matter of time before cocaine and other narcotics would follow. The man in charge was Francis Boots himself, who became a top priority for the Bangor, Maine, FBI office.

After interviewing many law enforcement officials and researching the Internet, I have concluded that segments of the Mohawk Warrior Society were the most militant organization involved in various criminal enterprises in most of North America. My evidence: The loss of revenue to Canada topped $1 billion because of the Warrior Society's involvement. There were massive shoot-outs. Militants always have guns. Those people had thousands of guns and they weren't afraid to use them.

The Abenaki (eastern) people, which includes the Passamaquoddy Tribe in Pleasant Point and Indian Township, Maine, are known collectively as People of the Dawn. In the Northeast, the People are made up of the Penobscots, the Passamaquoddy, the Maliseet, the Micmac and other tribes scattered throughout the region and parts of Quebec. Generally and historically, in contrast to the Mohawks, they have been a relatively peaceful people.

Over the centuries, Mohawks have tried to invade and control segments of the Wabanakis (the same as Abenakis). That's one of the reasons Fred Moore came forward. He feared a criminal takeover of the Pleasant Point Indian Reservation by the Mohawk Warrior Society, who, through Francis Boots, had shown interest in Passamaquoddy tribal territory. The Mohawks wanted to drive tractor-trailer loads of tobacco to Pleasant Point.

In early conversations with Fred, which came after Pierro initially contacted Anthony Stanley, Boots' representatives said they wanted to move 400 cases of tobacco from Pleasant Point to New Brunswick every week. They expected a profit of $300 per case times 400, or $120,000 per week, almost $6 million a year. Fred's cut would have been $20 per case, or $8,000 a week -- more than $400,000 a year in bribes. He was approached because of his navigational skills, but since he was the police chief, any money he was offered or given was a bribe under Maine law.

Armed with the Mohawk videotape and the intelligence, the FBI in Bangor made the smuggling scheme a matter of paramount concern. I was to be the point man and Fred would become the star witness. It was time to go operational.

After getting authorization from the FBI and Justice Department, as well as a commitment to prosecute by the U.S. Attorney's Office in Bangor, the case was opened. The case caption was "Francis Boots, War Chief, Mohawk Warrior Society, et al., Bribery, Fraud by Wire, and Interstate Transportation in aid to Racketeering."

Our task was to get a boat large enough to carry at least 50 cases of tobacco and smugglers across Passamaquoddy Bay. Each case weighed 14.3 pounds, so the total was 700 pounds-plus. On most nights, there were to be three smugglers, including Fred. After several phone calls, I located a seaworthy vessel owned by the Maine Marine Patrol (MMP). Sergeant Richard LeHaye of the MMP became my logistical contact.

In the interim, before the arrival of Boots and his people, I met with RCMP Corporal Randy Geddes and RCMP Constable Keith Larson. They would become my counterparts on the Canadian side of the border. We had a good initial meeting and set up communications and logistical plans.

We had obtained authority from the ambassadors to both countries to work in each other's country on a mutually beneficial case. Supervisory Special Agent Jim Powers from the Boston office, his squad and a surveillance squad from Boston (a total of 26 agents) would be coming to Calais to assist.

Powers was a short, wiry, powerful man with a desire to accomplish the Bureau's mission regardless of personal circumstances, a no-nonsense type. Jim had a degree in political science from Georgia Southern University, and entered the Bureau as a clerk in 1976. Before long, he became a criminal analyst and graduated from the FBI Academy as a special agent in 1982.

His first posting was to Salt Lake City, where he worked violent crimes. From 1984 to 1988, he worked undercover on a truck hijacking squad out of the Chicago office. While there, he "flipped" a Mafia guy who helped convict Chicago mob boss Sam Corlisi. Jim left Chicago in 1988 and went to FBI Headquarters as a supervisor on the applicant unit where he became the national recruiter of agents. In 1991, he was transferred to the Boston Division as a supervisor and picked up the Maine resident agencies as part of his assignment.

At the time Bangor opened operations in the Mohawk case, Jim supervised 26 agents and support personnel. He had his own squad, C-9, which handled bank failure investigations from 1991 to 1994.

In 1994, he was transferred to FBI Headquarters as inspector team leader.

Jim supported my every move on the Mohawk matter, as did the Assistant Special Agent in Charge of the Boston Criminal Division, Robert Conforti, and the Special Agent in Charge, Tom Hughes. Conforti ultimately became the Special Agent in Charge for the Philadelphia Division. He was another great agent and a great guy.

One of the immediate problems we encountered in the Calais and Perry, Maine, area was communications. Criminal elements of the Mohawk Warrior Society had tried to intercept police communications. There were virtually no communication systems that would support the FBI's secure frequencies or the RCMP secure frequencies. Agents could communicate car to car, but not at any great distance. As a result, Boston headquarters sent a communications team to Calais to hook up a temporary tower that extended our range. We provided the RCMP with a couple secure radios and they did the same for us.

Now we were ready. It took about a week for the FBI and RCMP to position ourselves since the initial meeting between Police Chief Moore, Anthony "Pluto" Stanley, Elwyn Cook and Dewey Lazore, which occurred on April 15, 1992. (To recap, Cook and Lazore were members of the Francis Boots organization. They were also co-owners of the tobacco.)

On April 23, 1992, five of us -- Corporal Geddes, Constable Larson, the FBI's Jim Powers, Police Chief Moore and myself -- visited St. Andrews, New Brunswick, to search for an off-loading point. We found one that was ideal at high tide on Bar Road, which went right down to the water. There was ample cover nearby for the RCMP surveillance units.

St. Paul, convert to Christianity and preacher to the Gentiles, was beheaded in the year 0067, the same day St. Peter was crucified. He died for the Greater Glory of God.

REFLECTIONS OF KEITH LARSON

On April 21, 1992, I took a phone call from the "J" Division at RCMP headquarters in Fredericton, New Brunswick, about meeting with an FBI agent named Don Goulet in regard to a possible tobacco smuggling operation generating from the Pleasant Point Reservation of the Passamaquoddy Tribe in eastern Maine. Needless to say, I was excited. On top of just being involved with the famed FBI was the possibility of a major illegal tobacco bust. At the time, the price of smokes in Canada was zooming and smuggling tobacco was a booming business.

In the months before April 1992, I was getting a lot of tips from informants and scoring tobacco arrests at a pretty good rate, about every two weeks or so. What HQ told me about my proposed meeting with Don in Calais, Maine, was a cop's total adrenaline rush thanks to the possibilities. I've always said to hell with cocaine; just do police work if you want a rush.

I met with Don at 8 p.m. one night. It was a long meeting. I didn't get home until 2:30 a.m. after beginning that day's shift at 8:30 a.m. The next day I briefed my superiors, then got a call from Don that Fred Moore had come up with a boat. It was a 16-foot Boston Whaler with a 35-horsepower outboard motor. My initial thought was that it was a tad small, but Passamaquoddy Bay can be friendly, especially at night.

On the afternoon of April 23, I met with the FBI surveillance team in Calais. I was totally impressed with their professionalism and enthusiasm, and they made it clear that Fred's safety was their primary concern. Working with the FBI, we tried to do some surveillance of Fred taking Pluto to look at off-loading sites in New Brunswick, specifically at Bar Road. But Murphy's Law prevailed and hit us with transmitter/reception problems.

Reviewing my police notebook, I see that I made a notation to myself with asterisks and exclamation marks: "Fred is an undercover agent and not an informant." That would have some bearing later on.

On April 24, I met with Fred in a motel room. It was a chance to see where this man was coming from. Man, did I get a quick education! I scribbled five pages of notes on his personal history, the Passamaqouddys, tribal beliefs, etc. He was totally open with me, and a bond began to form between us. This was an honorable man in whom integrity, a keen mind and honesty prevailed. I became a believer in Fred Moore and those feelings remain to this day.

Things were starting to move. Don and his boss from Boston, Jim Powers, kept me abreast of the illicit tobacco movement. The drop-off point on Bar Road wasn't a long haul from Maine and had a suitable beach for landing most smaller watercraft. (Actually, Bar Road is a bit famous thanks to the 25-plus feet of the Bay of Fundy tides. When the tide ebbs, you can literally drive to Ministers Island, an historic site with a millionaire's estate.) In any case, I checked the area out and found a suitable observation site about 150 yards from the shoreline in a stunted spruce thicket.

By this time, because I was a junior rank (constable), Corporal Randy Geddes from the Fredericton Federal Enforcement Section had been assigned the RCMP side of supervision. Randy is a wonderful, warm-hearted person with a keen mind and a great sense of humor, and I'm honored to call him a friend.

On May 2, they set up the first delivery of tobacco. Randy and I hid in the thicket, which gave us heavy concealment and a clear view of the shoreline. To our benefit, a streetlight a short distance away illuminated the scene -- unfortunately not enough to discern who was who, but enough to see activity clearly.

At 10:30 p.m., the suspect vehicle arrived. It was an older model Ford pickup with a cap on the box. We watched as two men paced the shoreline anticipating Fred's arrival. Along came Fred and his cronies at 12:48 a.m. They approached the beach cautiously until the keel gently touched the gravel.

Within seconds, the offload of illicit tobacco began. It consisted of 200-gram plastic bags stuffed into your typical green garbage bags. They unloaded about 50 bags at a very fast rate. Fred's job was done when the bags hit the beach and off he went, a mere 10 minutes later after arriving, while the targets scurried up and down the shore loading the truck. They left for Nova Scotia after about 10 more minutes

Finally, after all the intelligence-gathering and surveillance on targets, the first of a number of drops had happened. We had watched the arrival of the Mohawks before the first smuggle. When we knew the Mohawks were in town, we found out where they stayed and kept an eye on them.

I found myself putting in 12- to 16-hour days and loving it, but fatigue was setting in. As a result, many of my other case files lacked written entries even though I was still investigating them. What's more, I was preparing to help teach an Armed Ship Boarding Course in Halifax, Nova Scotia. So I relocated to my humble cabin in the woods to catch up on the paperwork and get a rest.

On April 23, Police Chief Moore and Anthony "Pluto" Stanley made a trip to the Bar Road location. Fred had been wired up to record the conversation with Pluto. While affixing the wire to Moore's upper torso, the FBI agents and RCMP officers saw the scars of wounds that Moore had suffered in several knifings. He had no less than eight scars on his stomach and chest. Here was a survivor and, apparently, a warrior.

The body wire proved to be fruitful as we got information from Pluto on his trip with Fred to St. Andrews that supported Moore's earlier description of the Mohawk game plan, as well as the identities of those involved.

We learned that Beverly Pierro and Jake Boots (Francis' brother) had been sent forward as an intelligence-gathering unit. They were due at the reservation on April 27 to review the smuggling plan with Moore and Pluto. We decided that Fred would take Pierro across the bay to the off-loading site. To do that, we borrowed a small, 16-foot Boston Whaler from the U.S. Coast Guard, which also loaned us cold weather gear.

On the April 27, Pierro, Jake Boots, Elwyn Cook and Dewey Lazore arrived at the reservation to review the smuggling plan. The next day, those four met with Moore and Pluto, and Pierro and Moore crossed Passamaquoddy Bay in the Whaler. The seas were rough and it was windy and cold. The distance was eight miles one way.

We had learned previously, through Pluto, that the tobacco smuggled into Canada would be going to the Eskazone Indian Reservation in Nova Scotia. The big honcho of tobacco smuggling in that part of the world was Stanley Johnson, also known to the RCMP as "The Fat Man." He was an Eskazone Indian.

The first smuggle happened on May 2, and Pluto was saying that Francis Boots, the man himself, might show up. Our operation involved 26 FBI agents and support personnel, as well as scores of RCMP officers and their support personnel. Both agencies had ample air coverage and at one point, a Night Stalker aircraft helped us out. Using infrared sensing, it could watch a man walking on the ground from an altitude of 10,000 feet.

That afternoon, we wired Fred up at the International Motel in Calais. He didn't appear to be nervous. He acted professionally and consistently demonstrated his commitment to the undercover operation. He returned to the reservation for a 7 p.m. meeting with the smugglers at Pluto's home. By that time, FBI agents had been placed in strategic locations inside and outside the reservation. I was in my Bureau car about 200 feet from Pluto's home with the intent of monitoring conversations. To avoid detection if anyone approached the vehicle, I was ready to lie down on the front seat.

There were no indications that the Mohawks and Pluto were trying to be careful about the security of their operation. They felt secure because they were on Indian territory and figured Fred had everything under control. At any sign of any trouble, all agents would be called in to help Fred. The ensuing conversations were recorded as well as transmitted to all cars that were equipped with receivers. Unfortunately, the transmitting device worked for just a couple hours before the battery wore out.

Francis Boots had indeed showed up and was doing a good job of hanging himself in what we monitored. They discussed Moore's police work and his knowledge of any patrol agencies working in the area. They also asked whether they could expect interference from the Passamaquoddy Police Department, and Fred said they wouldn't.

To our delight, the recorded conversation was devastating to everyone involved criminally. We learned that the Mohawks had brought 50 cases of tobacco from New York to be smuggled across Passamaquoddy Bay into St. Andrews, where the RCMP officers were set up.

So far, all had gone according to plan. The actual smuggling would begin at 9 p.m. The seas were rough and it was windy. But by 11 p.m., the 20-foot undercover Maine Marine Patrol boat (we had returned the Boston Whaler to the Coast Guard after we took Beverly Pierro across the bay because it was just too small for all the tobacco we expected it to carry) had not left Gleason's Cove in Perry, the jump-off point. I had forgotten to tell Chief Moore about the kill switch on the central panel of the boat, which had to be turned off for the engine to start. Ultimately, Moore figured that out.

In the interim, Powers got a bit worried. No longer having our transmitter going, thanks to worn-down batteries, we couldn't monitor exactly what was happening at Gleason's Cove. Powers came over the radio about 11 p.m. and asked to meet with me immediately. I drove to his location just off the reservation on Route One, and he said, "Donnie, the Mohawks have got Fred and they're cutting his balls off!"

I reassured Powers that Fred could take care of himself and control the situation. Calmed down a bit, Powers called a couple Maine FBI agents and asked them to drive to the Gleason's Cove area. One of them, D.B., said he didn't want to be the first agent to be tomahawked in Bureau history, which got a tension-busting laugh all around. D.B. and his partner left and checked out the cove and said the boat landing was still active.

Finally, about midnight, the boat was off to St. Andrews. The seas were still quite rough. On board were Pluto, Fred and Jake Boots. An hour and a half or so later, the RCMP radioed from the Bar Road area that they heard a boat approaching. By then, the wind had died down and fog covered the bay. Through almost impossible weather conditions, Fred had the guts and experience to pull it off. It helped that on the April 27 daylight trip with Pierro, he had marked all the details that he needed to make a safe trip at night. Also, Fred has fished the bay all his life and knew the crooks and crannies of the sometimes treacherous waters.

When Fred, Jake and Pluto reached the Canadian shore, two people jumped out of a waiting truck. One was large and portly. After the tobacco had been unloaded, he gave Jake a plastic bag full of money. Jake thumbed through the bills and told Fred it looked like it was all there.

Fred's return to the reservation was as nerve-wracking for us as the trip over. Since fog had enveloped the whole area, Fred had to carefully navigate a compass course, avoiding shoals and sand bars. He touched land about 3:30 a.m. Jake gave the money to his brother Francis Boots, who counted out $1,000 in two stacks of $20 bills, giving one to Fred and the other to Pluto. That satisfied the agreement of paying Fred $20 per case of tobacco smuggled, which Fred had decided to split evenly with Pluto.

In all, they had smuggled $15,000 back (the going rate was $300 per case) into the U.S., evading Customs, of course. Fred drove back to the International Hotel where he turned his share of the bribe money over to me as evidence. We counted it and put it in a plastic "valuable evidence" pouch. Two agents from Boston, Mark Little and Dennis Drum, took the money back to Boston. Mark and Dennis were good, young, enthusiastic agents who also handled the tape of the recorded conversations.

We didn't arrest anyone at the time because we didn't have authority from the U.S. Attorney's Office to do so. And we were in for the long haul. This was an undercover operation and the goal was to see how far we could penetrate the Mohawk Warrior Society, and to find out if there were other co-conspirators. Unlike police officers, the FBI usually will not make an arrest without approval from the U.S. Attorney's Office. In the smuggling case, the U.S. Attorney's Office wanted to present the facts to a federal grand jury.

Later that day, having debriefed Fred, the RCMP debriefed us. They said the portly man who met the boat was Stanley Johnson, Fat Man himself. That was great news. We had the main targets of the investigation in one smuggling attempt.

A few days earlier, more than 100 RCMP officers had raided Johnson's stores and warehouses, which were full of illegal tobacco.

He would store the tobacco in warehouses and then ship it to various store fronts and tobacco shops that he owned throughout the Maritime Provinces. His fronts were legitimate but much of the tobacco was not.

Before the smuggling, Johnson had made the front page of the Bangor Daily News by proclaiming that neither the RCMP, nor the FBI, nor the CIA could catch him. Because he was connected to Boots and because he was working with a corrupt Canadian public official, he felt safe involving himself in smuggling. The RCMP and the FBI kept a lid on the undercover sting operation and the information was strictly shared on a "need to know" basis. The Canadian public official who was already a target of the RCMP certainly would not have been made aware of this secretive undercover operation. Little did Johnson know that May 2 marked the beginning of the end of his criminal enterprise. It was a great day for law enforcement in both agencies.

(If I recall correctly, the RCMP didn't arrest Johnson after the raids because it had an extensive undercover long-term investigation going on.)

The next day, I sent a quick teletype to FBI Headquarters in Washington about a new "smuggling route [that] had been opened between the Passamaquoddy Reservation and St. Andrews, New Brunswick, which was controlled by the FBI on one side and by the RCMP on the other." Management was pleased with the results.

Ultimately, the operation provided probable cause for the RCMP to continue raiding various warehouses used by the Johnson enterprise in New Brunswick and Nova Scotia, eventually bringing him to his knees. After our operation was over, he was arrested and convicted and served two years in prison. The RCMP also arrested the mid- to high-level Canadian public official who was on the take and tipping Johnson about impending raids.

On May 3, I briefed Assistant U.S. Attorney Jim McCarthy on the criminal events that had occurred. But I had a gut feeling that his boss, U.S. Attorney Richard Cohen, did not want to prosecute. I felt the office was afraid of the Mohawk Warrior Society. Additionally, I believe the U.S. Attorney's Office did not want the FBI to come across certain connections that had been forged between federal officials and leaders of the Passamaquoddy tribe.

After the May 2 event, Chief Moore repeated the smuggling on May 10 and 16, June 1, 9 and 25, and Nov. 7. By then, Fred turned over to us $3,000 to $3,400 in bribe money that the Mohawks had given him.

After May 16, the FBI office at our embassy in Ottawa called Powers and told him that we should stop what we were doing because it had never been done internationally before. Powers response: "Well, we're doing it anyway." I had been in almost daily contact with the FBI Office of Liaison and International Affairs. We had the OK from them as well as permission from both Canadian and U.S. ambassadors.

Before the June 1 delivery of tobacco to the reservation by Dewey Lazore and his wife, the RCMP had cleaned out Johnson's warehouse and he needed to replenish his supplies. Lazore filled 30 plastic garbage bags with the equivalent of two cases of tobacco in each bag. On June 1, Fred traversed the bay alone, but there was no one at the St. Andrews off-load site to pick it up. Fred returned to the reservation and stored the tobacco in his home until June 9, when he took the load back over to St. Andrews.

On June 25, Fred delivered another load. The tobacco was driven to Nova Scotia for further distribution in the Maritime Provinces, including back into New Brunswick.

Eventually, Fred spoke with Beverly Pierro about the mix-up in a June 7 phone call. As with other conversations between the two of them, we recorded it. What we learned was that Johnson was low on money and wanted the Mohawks to front him the load of tobacco that had been sent on June 1, which was ultimately delivered on June 9. Chief Moore had decided before that call to cut Anthony "Pluto" Stanley out of the picture as he was usually quite intoxicated and Fred refused, for safety reasons, to bring him on any more trips across the bay. I agreed with Fred.

After the arrival of the June 1 load, I happened to be talking with Assistant U.S. Attorney McCarthy in his Bangor office. Assistant U.S. Attorney Jay P. McCloskey, who later replaced Richard Cohen as the United States Attorney, came into Jim's office and told me that he'd be taking over the Francis Boots investigation, as McCarthy was too busy to handle the matter.

Naturally, this added to my suspicion that the U.S. Attorney's Office never intended to prosecute this matter. McCarthy had been on the case for two months, and he knew the ins and outs of it. I told Powers of my suspicions, and he assured me that prosecution would happen. I added that Fred's credibility may have been the reason for any reluctance to prosecute, although I had always believed in his credibility. Right then, I decided to go undercover myself.

Somewhere around June 3, I went to Fred's home on the reservation, where he introduced me to Anthony Stanley as John Ames, an old acquaintance. I told Pluto that I was Fred's back-up. When I mentioned that I smelled a strong tobacco odor in the house, Pluto told Fred that I was a "hound dog," meaning I had a good nose. Pluto was in his early 40s, had a thin build and was an alcoholic. He had lived on the reservation his whole life.

I also told Pluto I had covered their backsides on the previous smuggling runs, that I was armed with an M-16 rifle and that I provided the boat used in the ventures. Pluto opened up immediately and told me a lot about who was involved on both sides of the border. He said he was contacted initially in early April by Beverly Pierro and Francis Boots, and that he then approached Fred.

He also mentioned his affiliation with Boots in the 1970s during a Native American sit-in at the Akwesasne Indian Reservation. All the pieces fell into place and Fred's credibility could no longer be an issue. I had brought six lobsters and a six-pack of Miller beer to share with Pluto and Fred. They cost the government $54, a bargain considering what I learned that day.

Throughout the smuggling period, the FBI and RCMP controlled the time and place of every venture. We dictated through Fred when the Mohawks should come and when they should not.

On June 9, the tobacco from Fred's house that had been packaged in dark green plastic bags (the tobacco that Fred brought back from his abortive smuggling attempt) was delivered by Fred to the Stanley Johnson organization. Fred got $1,200 for his effort, and like all other such occasions, turned it over to the FBI.

During the middle of May or early June, I learned through the FBI that a major espionage investigation was underway in the Bangor area. It involved a serviceman stationed there. That's all I knew as this sort of intelligence was always compartmentalized -- the fewer people in on it, the lower the chances of a security breach. So I didn't ask any questions.

In the middle of June, after my son Keith graduated from John Bapst High School with the eventual intent of going to medical school, I called the Army recruiter in Bangor to find out what college programs might be available through the military. I didn't know it at the time, but the main target of the espionage investigation in Bangor was the Army's recruiting sergeant.

You could surmise that I probably called a phone number that was under surveillance by whoever was heading the investigation for the military. A call placed to the Army recruiting number by an FBI agent probably raised a few eyebrows.

The next thing I knew, my sixth sense told me I was being followed, but I can never be sure that was the case. At the time, the movie "Thunderheart," starring Val Kilmer, had made its debut. He was an FBI agent probing corruption on an Indian reservation. John Anderson's song "Seminole Wind" was released about the same time.

Meanwhile, the smuggling runs went on and on because the U.S. Attorney's Office was dragging its feet and would not allow arrests and would not commit to prosecution. Additionally, it was a deep cover undercover operation and we had goals besides the tobacco smuggling, such as going undercover on the Akwesasne Indian Reservation and finding out who may have shot down an Air National Guard helicopter in 1992 and who had killed Corporal Marcel LeMay at the Oka shoot-out. What's more, we didn't know who might show up to help with the smuggling. So it was a long-term operation, not a one-time sting.

The Akwesasne Reservation was a dangerous place to work undercover, but Fred and I were committed to trying it. Our efforts were to no avail because the commanding officer of the Royal Canadian Mounted Police in Quebec Province said he could not guarantee our safety and stopped the initiative.

After the June 25 smuggling run, we decided to slow down the ventures so that everyone could catch their breath on both sides of the border. Fred and I had 65 or so recorded conversations that needed to be transcribed. The transcription was handled by two or three stenographers in the Boston office, and they did a superb job.

In late June or early July, I asked my old friend, retired Game Warden Bill Downing, if he could recommend a camp for Fred and I to stay in secretly while we reviewed the transcripts of the tapes. He put me in touch with a supervisory game warden who gave us permission to use a camp off Route 6 up on East Musquash Lake near Topsfield, Maine. Only Fred, myself, the game warden supervisor, Bill Downing, FBI Agent Powers and my partner in Bangor, J.S, knew its location.

I arranged to call Powers every day at 10 a.m. during the week to provide progress reports and let him know of any potential safety problems. Since the investigation began, Fred had reported being followed, and both the Bangor Daily News and I got many calls alleging that Fred was smuggling drugs or had used marijuana years ago. It had been quite apparent that several people were interested in what Fred and I were doing, and many tried to discredit him. I wondered why. I also wondered how they linked Fred and I since we had kept -- or thought we had kept -- a lid on the investigation.

Fred and I drove in early July from my house in Brewer to the East Musquash Lake hideout using my personal pickup truck, a gray 1986 Ford 150. We arrived on the weekend, unloaded our gear and set up our electronic equipment to transcribe, dictate and review tapes that hadn't gone through the FBI stenographers.

It went well. We worked 10- to 12-hours days, and each evening we fished the lake for pickerel and lake trout. We fished for one or two hours, had a drink and retired for the night, only to start the same process the next day.

On the following Thursday, Fred and I were driving back to camp on Route 6. The pay phone that we used to call Powers was in Topsfield, north of us. Close to camp, I spotted a helicopter flying at tree-top level about a quarter-mile away heading north along Route 6, opposite our direction. I soon heard the *whup whup* of chopper blades.

Instinctively, I just knew they were searching for us. We made a right hand turn onto the dirt road leading to our cabin when the chopper flew over and tilted to the right. Fred said he saw someone photograph us. That's all we needed -- to be placed under surveillance by our own military. The timing of the fly-over was exact and no one knew about our 10 a.m. schedule except for Powers. He told me he knew nothing about it and I believed him.

The following week, after I worked on other cases in Bangor, I returned home and my wife was pretty upset. She said a sedan with two men sitting in it wearing white shirts had had the house under surveillance. They had watched the house for about a half-hour.

She was alone at home with my youngest daughter, Kristen. Eventually, she approached the sedan, which sped off. The same day, a helicopter flew overhead so close to the house that she waved at a crewmember who was hanging out of the door. What the hell was going on?

Meanwhile, Fred had been placed on paid suspension by tribal governor Cliv Dore pending an investigation into his conduct. When Pluto was removed from the smuggling operation, he had approached the Passamaquoddy Tribal Council and told them Fred was smuggling tobacco with the Mohawks.

Fred said that Dore suspected him of keeping him, the tribal governor, under surveillance or investigation for public corruption, which is why Dore ultimately fired him as police chief. Throughout the Mohawk investigation, I became increasingly concerned about the relationship that the tribal governors and one of the tribe's attorneys, Tom Tureen, may have had with U.S. Attorney Richard Cohen. Tureen had suggested to Robert Newell, the Indian Township Reservation chief, and Cliv Dore that they fired Fred because he did not follow the police manual.

I had learned that Cohen and Tureen were extremely close. At the time, there was a push to establish a reservation-owned casino. Sure enough, sometime after Cohen left office, in the summer of 1993, he went to work for the tribe as a paid consultant on the casino. But the voters of Maine rejected a casino bill in 1994.

Clearly, I thought the Mohawk case would show that Police Chief Moore was a public official and that receiving anything of value from the Mohawks constituted bribery had he overlooked their wrongdoing. As far as I'm concerned, the same standards (a law, actually) should apply to other public officials associated with the reservation or other governmental entities.

Was the Mohawk case jeopardizing other criminal wrongdoing related to the tribe and its programs and investments? That was never answered. Were Fred and I running against the wind? It sure looked like it.

Early in the Boots matter, the Office of the Inspector General for Investigations (OIG) at the U.S. Department of the Interior and the FBI received many allegations of wrongdoing, possibly involving attorneys representing the Passamaquoddy and Penobscot tribes. The allegations ranged from providing kickbacks to tribal governors and conflict of interest in a matter identified as Passamaquoddy Technology.

Passamaquoddy Technology was a business venture entered into by the tribe as a limited partner -- with Thomas Tureen the president and others as general partners -- to create, research and develop an environmental scrubber for the cement industry. The scrubber technology would take out noxious particulates from smoke stack emissions and transform them into precipitates that could, we were told, be sold to fertilizer companies.

The tribe put up most of the money -- about $9 million total, including $2.5 million in tribal money and $6.5 million loaned by BIA to the tribe -- to help fund the project. Charles "Chuck" Gifford, a senior special agent at Interior's IG, helped me on the matter. He had great insight into Native American matters as well as a tremendous working knowledge of Bureau of Indian Affairs loans and grants.

Gifford was a native Mainer, four years my senior. He was born in Old Town and graduated from the University of Maine in 1976 with an associate's degree in criminal justice. He served with the Air Force from 1961 until 1965, when he became a Maine state trooper. He served in the "County" (Aroostook County) until 1972, when he was named a U.S. Treasury agent with the Internal Revenue Service (IRS) in Boston.

In 1974, he became a criminal investigator for the U.S. Department of Energy in Bangor and later in Washington. In 1979, he joined the Inspector General at Interior and stayed there until he retired in 1998. At one point in his IG career he was offered the position of Special Agent in Charge in Sacramento, Calif., but refused the promotion because he loved "working the streets," conducting criminal investigations, as I did. We got along very well.

Over the next several years, Chuck and I investigated many allegations. Most were minor and involved only conflict-of-interest issues. But the Passamaquoddy Technology matter was different. If you include construction costs of the scrubber, more than $15 million in federal and tribal funds had been used for the project.

The scrubber is at the Dragon Cement plant in Thomaston, Maine. Of that $15 million, about $6.5 million went into research and development. But various Passamaquoddy residents made allegations ranging from fraud against the government to kickbacks from P-Tech to former tribal governors.

The FBI decided in 1995 to transfer the case to our Washington Field Office inasmuch as the primary victim might be the Bureau of Indian Affairs, which was just across the Potomac River in Alexandria, Virginia. There the case suffered a slow death for various reasons, including my personal failure, meaning my breakdown.

Not one subpoenaed record or any FD-302 (an FBI agent's written report of interview) was submitted to a grand jury. The case was closed on a technicality (which I can't discuss further) when my mental illness and alcohol dependence overwhelmed me. Chuck, myself and the Washington Field Office agents had given this matter our best shot. Life went on.

Let's get back to the Mohawk case. Police Chief Fred Moore was permanently fired from his position in late August of 1992. Tribal governors, Cliv Dore of Pleasant Point, and Indian Township Governor Robert Newell had, on the advice of the tribe's attorney, dismissed him for not following "the police manual." The real reason was that Dore believed Fred was investigating him. Then Pluto's allegation that Fred was smuggling illegal tobacco with the Mohawks gave them the opening to fire him.

The FBI stood up for him all the way. But we could not intercede with the tribal governors as the undercover operation was still underway, and the tribal governors could have contacted the Mohawk Warriors and tipped them about it. Besides, after Fred was fired, he no longer wanted to be reservation police chief. The Bureau of Indian Affairs offered him work in various states throughout the country, and the FBI was willing to help set that up, but Fred elected to stay on the rez.

As a result, Fred was strapped for cash. At one point, he told me he was catching mackerel and selling them for 50 cents apiece to buy hot dogs for his children. At that juncture, the Bureau stepped in and gave him temporary income of about $350 a week, equal to what he made as a police chief. After the active portion of the investigation and other investigations were concluded, when his life was in danger, the FBI gave him $25,000. He and his family spent a week at Disney World and stayed in Florida for several more weeks.

During the peak of the Boots investigation in late July or early August, I decided to take three days off to be with my family. We planned on visiting friends in Seymour, Conn., our old neighborhood. Meanwhile, I had been complaining to the FBI in Boston about the surveillance of Fred and myself, but the Bureau never responded.

My family, Donna and the three kids and I, left Brewer on a Friday morning. I had a gut feeling that something wasn't right. Sure enough, while driving on I-84 through Massachusetts and into Connecticut, I noticed that we were being followed. The first indication was a sedan that passed us on the right. The driver was talking on a radio and the car bore a tag number that was an exact match for the acronym of the Bureau's secret radio system. I think they were testing me and my observation skills.

At the next exit, I pulled off the highway, drove to a safe area and scanned the skies for any Bureau aircraft that might have us under surveillance. I re-entered the highway and several minutes later, I spotted Jim Powers pass me on the left in a blue Chevrolet Caprice. I knew then and there that we were truly under surveillance. Not only did I have to watch out for the bad guys, but also the good guys *and* the military. I had been in Bangor only nine months.

As we approached our destination, I told Donna to expect the FBI to interrupt our vacation within 15 minutes. Sure enough, after we got to our friend's house, there was a knock on the door and Powers and a female agent asked to come in. They came in and Powers ordered me, without giving any reason, to go to the FBI office in Hartford, Connecticut, which I did. He and the female agent stayed behind and interviewed Donna. My family and friends were extremely upset. Donna was deeply disappointed in the Bureau.

At the Hartford office, I saw an old friend of mine from the Bureau Academy days, John Lewis. We spoke briefly. The Boston Special Agent in Charge, Thomas Hughes, then entered the room. He asked me to leave my weapon with him and told me to go to an inner office where a female psychologist or psychiatrist from Washington, D.C. was waiting.

We had a two-hour conversation about possible PTSD (post-traumatic stress disorder), alcohol consumption, and what was transpiring in Bangor. I told her everything, including the surveillance of my home when I was away. I also said I drank alcohol during my down time. She was satisfied with my responses and I was returned to full duty. I had never done a single thing wrong.

After the meeting, Hughes told me, "You're pretty smart. Goddamn it, Goulet, don't let me down." I told him I wouldn't, but I was pretty pissed off. I figured that if they had a problem with me, they could have handled it differently without involving my family members and friends, placing us under surveillance the way they did.

A couple days after I got back to Bangor, Powers called and apologized for the trauma my family and I had been put through. I accepted his apology. Years later, he told me that FBI Headquarters had taken over the personnel matter and called all the shots.

So it was back to the streets. Fred, Chuck and I had some big fish to fry.

In late August 1992, after detailed discussion with Assistant U.S. Attorney Jay McCloskey, the FBI was promised prosecution of the Boots matter. I called a meeting in Bangor of all law enforcement managers who would be involved in the arrests. Twelve supervisors and managers attended the meeting. They were from the FBI, Albany Division; FBI, Boston; New York State Police; and the RCMP.

McCloskey would not allow Fred to attend the meeting, perhaps because he wanted to gain control of the investigation. During the meeting, which McCloskey attended, we were told that by the end of the following week, arrest warrants would be issued for each member of the conspiracy. The charges would be bribery and failure to report currency transactions internationally (by law, you cannot take more than $10,000 into or out of the country without filing a monetary report with Customs. It's a felony punishable by up to five years in prison), as well as violations of the Interstate Transportation in Aid to Racketeering Act. The counts involving fraud by wire against a foreign government would not be brought by the U.S. Attorney's Office.

We set an arrest date for the following Friday and called off the smuggling ventures. I periodically checked with McCloskey during the following week. On Thursday, the day before the warrants were to come out, Fred and I went to the U.S. Attorney's Office, where McCloskey was to brief us on the arrest warrants.

As we entered the building, Assistant U.S. Attorney Tim Wing passed on his way out. With a smirking sort of smile, he looked right at me. I knew right then that McCloskey wasn't going to prosecute. A few minutes later, McCloskey's office confirmed my suspicions. I asked him why not and he said he had a problem with Fred's credibility.

I was livid. All over the Northeast, law enforcements officers were gearing up for arrests the following day and McCloskey pulled this on us. Fred said I turned red as a beet. I left McCloskey's office and told him Fred was not to go anywhere until my return.

Back at my office, I called Powers in Boston. He was incredulous and told me to stay in my office until he called back. After about a half-hour, he called and said, "It's okay. McCloskey will prosecute." I walked back to Jay's office. Apparently he had been subdued. He sat there for minutes with his head down while Fred and I patiently waited for some action.

Then he straightened up, pulled the complete case file and started going over every single detail of the operation. He was finally on board. All three of us rolled up our sleeves and worked together professionally for the next several months.

I never found out what Powers did to reverse McCloskey's decision. I suspect it went up the ladder, probably all the way up to the director of the FBI. I can't be certain of that, but who ever talked with McCloskey brought him on board real quick.

Since we couldn't make arrests then (we had to go over the whole case again because McCloskey had left out key points needed for indictments and trials), Fred and I had to keep the undercover operation going to keep from tipping off the Mohawks. We set up a smuggling run through Beverly and Jake on Nov. 7. On that day, Fred crossed Passamaquoddy Bay with Jake Boots. The sea was gray and angry and it was bitterly cold and windy. When they got back, their boat was covered with ice, as were Fred and Jake. I decided then and there to end the undercover operation. The going was just too tough.

The Mohawks must have been very pleased with the results because apparently other smugglers had heard about the route. In early December of 1992, Anthony "Pluto" Stanley got a call from a Native American at the St. Regis Reservation in upstate New York. He told Fred that another group wanted him to smuggle tobacco into Canada. Pluto named a Louis Tarbell and a Charles "Chuck" Mancuso from Buffalo, New York

We decided to accommodate them. However, this time, we smuggled the tobacco overland into Canada and not by sea. I contacted an old RCMP friend of mine, Greg McAvoy. We arranged a small undercover sting operation. Fred drove a pickup loaded with tobacco to the Milltown crossing north of St. Stephen, New Brunswick, across from Calais, Maine. At the Canadian Customs Port of Entry, an undercover RCMP officer took control of the pickup and delivered the goods to the recipient.

I don't recall who the recipient was as it happened 30 miles from the U.S. border and the RCMP handled that aspect of it up there. Upon delivery, police seized the tobacco and the funds that were to have paid for it.

Before that, Fred had made arrangements with Mancuso and Tarbell, who arrived in Calais at the same time as the load. They stayed at the Calais Motor Inn. Fred and I stayed three rooms down from their room. (I wasn't afraid of being spotted with Fred because I was working undercover under the alias of John Ames, so I was prepared to enter any undercover operation.)

We recorded their conversations. After delivery of the load, Fred was supposed to return with the funds, smuggling them through U.S. Customs and giving most if it, minus his take, to Mancuso and Tarbell. Fred's take would have been $1,000. I think the total was around $20,000 for about 60 cases of tobacco.

After the load was "smuggled" through Canadian Customs and ultimately seized by the RCMP, Fred called Mancuso and told him that he didn't have any money to bring back. Mancuso was furious. Fred and I then checked out of the motel for our own safety and went to Bangor, where we called and recorded subsequent Mancuso responses.

Mancuso said, "Fred, where's the money? You don't know who you're dealing with." Fred said, "I don't have it." Then Mancuso said something to the effect that if he returned to New York without any money, "they" were going to break his legs and then he'd have to return to Maine and break Fred's legs.

It was time to shut the whole operation down. Heavily armed U.S. Border Patrol agents escorted Fred and his family from the reservation the following day. Fred went to Boston on the first leg of his family's trip to Florida.

On January 20, 1993, we arrested the Mohawks -- Jake Boots, Francis Boots, Dewey Lazore, Beverly Pierro and Ellwyn Cook, as well as Pluto. Additionally, Stanley Johnson from Nova Scotia was indicted as a co-conspirator. None of them resisted as they were taken into custody by a consortium of FBI agents, New York State Police and Washington County (Maine) Sheriff's Department deputies. They were all very surprised. When I arrested Anthony Stanley on the reservation, he was bitterly angry with Fred and he was scared. Tarbell and Mancuso ended up being charged separately by the U.S. Attorney's Office in Portland, Maine. They pleaded guilty to conspiracy, unlawful possession of untaxed cigarettes and the Federal Travel Act.

On January 19, 1993, the U.S. Attorney's Office in Bangor filed a 21-count indictment, naming the Mohawks and the others, including Stanley Johnson, the Fat Man. Counting Mancuso and Tarbell, the number of people charged in the United States was nine. The RCMP had already charged 24 people throughout Canada on July 8, 1992.

On July 9, 1992, the Daily News in Halifax, Nova Scotia, ran an article saying that 24 people in Canada were charged with smuggling and defrauding the provincial government of Nova Scotia. Former RCMP Officer Wayne Chesley Lacey was one of those indicted in 47 charges, including bribing a government official and obstruction of justice. Lacey had been a veteran RCMP officer based in Halifax, retiring a couple years before the article ran to take a job as an auditor in the Fuel and Tobacco Tax Division in the Finance Department.

Lacey was accused of taking bribe money from Clarence Gould, who was acting for the RCMP at the time. Other notable individuals charged were Stanley Gordon Johnson (Fat Man), who was a main subject of the FBI investigation in Maine. Also charged were Marion Murdock, David Calvin Naugle, Edward Googoo and several others.

The FBI investigation that was launched in April of 1992, thanks to Fred Moore, dovetailed into the RCMP investigation, which had been underway since July of 1991. We were able to provide probable cause for that investigation, which resulted in some of the charges.

Back to the Mohawk case, the U.S. indictment in January 1993 cited the Fraud by Wire statute, naming the government of Canada as the victim. It also named the Passamaquoddy people as victims, citing the Interstate Transportation in Aid to Racketeering statute (bribery), failure to report currency and monetary instruments, false statements, mail fraud and a conspiracy count for each defendant.

Anticipating a potential uprising by the Warriors and their sympathizers on the Akwesasne Reservation, the Canadian armed forces had placed 5,000 troops on standby during the arrest period. The night of the arrest, the Mohawk Warriors held a war dance. But nothing further developed.

As I noted earlier, the Fraud by Wire statute, Title 18, United States Code, Section 1343, had never been used successfully before with a foreign government being the victim. So this was indeed precedent-setting. The U.S. District Court in Bangor set a trial date of January 30, 1994.

Going back to October of 1992, the espionage case that I mentioned earlier came to public light. The main target of the investigation in Bangor was Jeffrey Stephen Rondeau, the local Army recruiter in Bangor. He was arrested in Florida on Oct. 22. On that day, the FBI asked me to keep an eye on Rondeau's residence. I watched his house and notified other agents when he left, destined for Florida. I'm sure it was consolation for me from the Bureau for what my family and I had been through earlier in the year. The FBI thanked me in a letter for helping apprehend Rondeau.

Rondeau had been part of a group organized by former Sgt. Clyde Lee Conrad that provided Army and NATO defense secrets, including tactical nuclear weapon plans, to intelligence agents of Hungary and Czechoslovakia from 1985 through 1988. In June of 1994, a military court sentenced Rondeau to 18 years in prison.

CHAPTER 8

THE TRIAL

(JANUARY 28, 1994)

St. John the Baptist, last of the prophets, exclaimed, "Behold the Lamb of God who takes away the sins of the world" as he pointed to Jesus. St. John was beheaded by Herod Antipas one year before the death of Christ. He died for the Greater Glory of God.

One year earlier, the arrests of Francis Boots, et al., had occurred. It was time for the trial to begin. U.S. District Court Judge Morton A. Brody presided. Newly appointed U.S. Attorney Jay P. McCloskey argued the government's case. Defendant Ellwyn Cook was represented by Michael Sawiki, of Buffalo, N.Y. Dewey Lazore was represented by Perry O'Brien from Bangor. Francis Boots was represented by Sandra B. Dombro of Bangor. Jake Boots was represented by J. Hillary Billings of Bangor. Beverly Pierro was represented by James Munch of Bangor.

After the first day of the trial, Beverly Pierro and Jake Boots pled guilty to smuggling currency in excess of $10,000 back into the U.S.

and failure to report the currency on a U.S. Customs baggage declaration. Both received eight-month sentences in a federal penitentiary. Anthony "Pluto" Stanley cooperated with the government and testified against all of the other defendants. He was also given an eight-month sentence. A diabetic, he recently died of complications from the disease.

That left Francis Boots, Dewey Lazore and Ellwyn Cook to be tried by a jury of 12. A year earlier, a 21-count indictment against the co-conspirators had been returned by a federal grand jury. The major crimes charged were: Interstate Transportation in Aid to Racketeering (bribery was the offense) and fraud by wire with the Canadian government being the victim, in which interstate phone calls had been made to further the scheme to defraud.

Also cited was a mail fraud count alleging that U.S. mail was used to forward a bribe payment to Fred Moore from Beverly Pierro at the St. Regis Reservation. Additionally, fraud by wire charges named the Pleasant Point Passamaquoddy Indians as victims. Finally, all the defendants were charged with conspiracy.

Defense counsel raised numerous issues in an attempt to impeach Fred Moore's testimony. Judge Brody ruled against the defense on the important issues. For example, defense wanted to present Fred's criminal record to show he was not credible. But since the crimes had occurred more than 10 years earlier and Fred had received a governor's pardon for that earlier assault, Judge Brody ruled that the defense could not inform the jury of this offense. He ruled that it would be unnecessarily prejudicial. Additionally, the crime of assault does not involve moral turpitude, according to the judge.

Throughout the trial, Fred was hammered incessantly by the defense lawyers who sought to discredit him and trip him up. But he responded truthfully to every question.

Pluto testified for about four hours, outlining the Mohawk plan as Pierro presented it to him almost two years earlier. When asked to identify Francis Boots, Dewey Lazore and Ellwyn Cook, Pluto did so accurately.

I testified for about four hours, bringing in the tapes that Fred and I had recorded -- more than 67 of them -- as evidence. They were devastating to the defense.

A Canadian Customs official, Dougal Kennedy, also testified for about four hours, focusing on the loss of revenue Canada suffered from the tobacco smuggled during the undercover operation. Because of the smuggling scheme, Canada realized a total loss of about $250,000.

There were a couple of interesting developments during the trial. One was the sprinkling of "sacred" tobacco throughout the courtroom on the third or fourth day of the trial. Apparently, Mohawk family members and friends who attended the trial dispersed the substance to influence the court and prove that tobacco was held "sacred" by the Mohawk people.

Another interesting sidelight was Ellwyn Cook's appearance on the last day of the trial wearing nothing but a loincloth. Cook was a pretty big guy and his appearance in that get-up brought many secretaries out of their offices to take a closer look. That day, about 40 visitors entered the courtroom to see Cook.

After listening to six days of testimony and the tapes, the jury retired. They deliberated for six to eight hours and returned guilty verdicts on all counts against the three remaining defendants, including "devising a scheme or artifice to deprive the residents of the Passamaquoddy Reservation in Maine of <u>the honest services of their police chief</u>, in violation of Title 18, United States Code, Sections 1343 and 1346."

All three of the defendants were sentenced to 24 months in a federal penitentiary and were released on their own recognizance. Francis Boots and Dewey Lazore eventually reported to prison, but Ellwyn Cook did not and he remains a fugitive to this day, living on the Canadian side of the Akwesasne Indian Reservation.

The guilty verdicts affirmed what many honest traditional Mohawk people had repeatedly pointed out over the years, that the Mohawk Warriors were involved in tobacco and cigarette smuggling. Additionally, Francis Boots, the War Chief of the Society, was "de-horned" (removed from office) a few months after the trial. Also, those convicted are not allowed to possess guns in the United States.

The evening after the verdicts, Fred and I and McCloskey went to a local restaurant and had a couple beers. McCloskey commended me for a job well done and congratulated Fred, calling him one of the best witnesses he had ever encountered in a trial.

The results were a huge accomplishment for the RCMP and the FBI. Without the heroic acts of former Police Chief Frederick Moore, none of it would have been possible. He was given a letter of commendation by FBI Director Louis Freeh and a plaque featuring an eagle and words praising him for his efforts as a true hero.

But the case was not over yet as the convicted Mohawks appealed the verdict to the U.S. First Circuit Court of Appeals in Boston.

Chesuncook

U.S. Department of Justice

Federal Bureau of Investigation

Office of the Director

Washington, D.C. 20535

November 28, 1994

Mr. Frederick Moore III
Pleasant Point Indian Reservation
Perry, Maine

Dear Mr. Moore:

    I want to extend the FBI's gratitude for your willingness to assist representatives of our Boston Office in connection with a major international corruption investigation involving Francis Boots, War Chief of the Mohawk Warrior Society, and others.

    My associates in Boston have advised that while performing your official duties as the former Pleasant Point Chief of Police, you placed yourself in extreme physical peril, suffered frenetic attempts to publicly discredit you, and were fired from your job by those you sought to protect from criminal influence. These extraordinary sacrifices on behalf of law enforcement and the citizens of Canada and the United States deserve the highest form of recognition. You can take great pride in knowing that your excellent efforts contributed substantially to successful prosecutions in Canada and the United States.

    In addition to acknowledging your tremendous help in the Boots case, I want to congratulate you on your recent election as tribal representative of the Passamaquoddy Tribe to the Maine legislature. I hope the future brings you every happiness and success.

Sincerely yours,

Louis J. Freeh
Director

CHAPTER 9

CONFLICTS IN THE COURTS (THE BOOTS, TRAPILO AND PASQUANTINO CASES)

St. Andrew, the brother of St. Peter, was scourged to death and preached for two days while dying in 0061. He died for the Greater Glory of God.

As I said earlier, the Boots matter was a pioneering case that tested the Fraud by Wire statute as it applied to a foreign government being the victim. It states: "Whoever, having devised or intending to devise a scheme or artifice to defraud, or for obtaining money or property by means of false or fraudulent pretenses, representations, or promises, transmits or causes to be transmitted, by means of wire communication in interstate or foreign commerce, any writings, signs, signal, pictures or sounds for the purpose of executing such a scheme or artifice, shall be fined under this title or imprisoned not more than five years or both."

Defendants Lazore, Cook and Francis Boots petitioned the First Circuit Court of Appeals in Boston, which reversed U.S. District Judge Brody's decision that the Fraud by Wire statute was relevant in the case. The government appealed to the Supreme Court, which declined to take the case. Those of us who'd been involved in the case weren't all that upset about it. We had done our jobs and done them well, and we hoped the courts would eventually rule in our favor.

When it involves a foreign country, there must be a reciprocal agreement before smuggling charges can be brought and the smuggling can only be made by vessel. (There is no anti-smuggling statute for smuggling by car. There is no reciprocal agreement with Canada.) That's why the Fraud by Wire statute has been such an important new tool for law enforcement.

On February 29, 1996, the U.S. filed a one-count indictment charging Robert Trapilo and three others with a money laundering conspiracy alleging that they conspired to engage in a series of financial transactions aimed a defrauding the Canadian government of tax revenue in violation of the wire fraud statute.

But the U.S. District Court for the Northern District of New York adopted the First Circuit Court of Appeals reasoning in the U.S. v. Boots case that a scheme to defraud a foreign government is not prosecutable under the Fraud by Wire statute because the "revenue rule" may apply. The revenue rule is an old common law rule whereby one country is prohibited from enforcing the revenue rules of another country, and it's fairly simple. So the District Court dismissed the indictment.

The government appealed again, this time to the Second U.S. Circuit Court of Appeals in New York, arguing that the wire fraud statute condemns any fraud where any interstate or foreign telecommunications systems are used and does not require the court to determine the validity of Canadian tax law. That court agreed and remanded the case to the

District Court for further proceedings. The defendants appealed one step higher because of the conflicting judicial decisions, but the Supreme Court declined to take the case.

Then another case, called Pasquantino, went to the Fourth Circuit Court of Appeals in Maryland. David Pasquantino and two others were convicted of using interstate wires to defraud Canada and the province of Ontario of excise duties and tax revenues relating to the importation and sale of liquor. They had ordered liquor by phone from discount stores in Maryland and ultimately smuggled the liquor into Canada in the trunks of cars. This scheme persisted for four years until they were apprehended in May 2000.

By smuggling, they had avoided paying Canadian taxes and duties worth $3.6 million in U.S. dollars. Pasquantino and his cohorts were convicted of wire fraud in U.S. District Court in Maryland, naming Canada as victim. On appeal by the defendants, a divided panel of the Court of Appeals then reversed the convictions.

The U.S. asked for a decision by the complete Court of Appeals for the Fourth District. It ruled 9-2 that the District Court convictions were valid. The defendants appealed to the Supreme Court, and this time the justices agreed in April 2004 to take the case.

A year, later Justice Clarence Thomas, supported by four of his colleagues, wrote, "...at common law, the revenue rule generally barred courts from enforcing the tax laws of foreign sovereigns. The question presented in this case is whether a plot to defraud a foreign government of tax revenue violates the federal wire fraud statute...Because...this construction of the wire fraud statute does not derogate from the common law revenue rule, we hold that it does." That judgment upheld the convictions of the Pasquantino group.

Anyone interested in more detailed information on arguments in this matter can check out the following on the Internet: Pasquantino, United States v. Francis Boots, United States v. Trapilo.

The Supreme Court's affirmation of the Fraud by Wire statute in smuggling cases is expected to deter attempts to smuggle goods into a foreign country. That court victory is international in scope and is designed to prevent domestic-based criminal organizations from smuggling high-tariff goods into foreign countries. Naturally, attorneys on the other side, particularly from the corporate world, have criticized the ruling.

Be that as it may, it is now the law of the land and Fred and I are honored to have been involved in the case that spearheaded use of the Fraud by Wire statute in 1992. No longer can criminal groups based in the U.S. be immune from the Fraud by Wire statute if they smuggle goods into foreign countries and use telecommunications systems to further their schemes. It was a great victory for Canada and the United States, and will continue to strengthen the relationship between law enforcement agencies in the U.S. and foreign governments, particularly at a time when terrorism is such a threat.

What it comes down to is this: Before the courts upheld the Fraud by Wire statute the way they did, smuggling goods from the United States into Canada wasn't prosecutable in the United States.

CHAPTER 10

THE MANIFESTATIONS OF MENTAL DISORDERS

St. Simon, brother to St. Jude, was crucified for his Christianity in the year 0067. He died for the Greater Glory of God.

In 1992, 1993, 1994, 1995 and 1996, my superiors consistently gave me an overall "exceptional" performance evaluation. I worked the cases that came my way with diligence and enthusiasm. Had I been alcohol-dependent, I could never have achieved those successes. However, as we'll see, things began to change for the worse in 1997.

In the fall of 1996 and winter of 1997, I played hockey on a local men's team at Alfond Arena at the University of Maine in Orono. One of my teammates was my FBI partner, W.H. I was 50 years old. My reflexes were off a bit and I didn't have the stamina I once had, but I was still fit enough to compete.

Toward the end of one game, I felt a deep sharp pain in the center of my chest accompanied by dizziness, heavy-headedness and pain in my head. So I quit hockey. I should have gone to the doctor immediately, of course, but pride kept me from making that obvious move.

Over the next several months, the heavy-headedness manifested itself every time I walked into a grocery store or mall stores. The fluorescent lights triggered what I could only call "head pressure" and I had to squint my eyes. And while in the store, I had trouble concentrating. Once I left, the pressure and squinting were alleviated and my concentration returned.

Over the next year, my mental status changed as I began to feel anxious and a bit concerned about my performance. The head pressure and squinting increased dramatically, particularly as a result of work-related stress. No longer were the symptoms related to fluorescent lighting alone. Something else was happening. I wasn't certain what it was, but I thought I could find relief in rest and relaxation.

In the late winter and early spring of 1997, I got involved in a substantial sensitive matter that I can't discuss today. The investigative findings led me to conclude that it could lead to the death of several innocent people if not handled properly. I presented my findings and conclusions to Boston management for direction.

But they couldn't help me, as apparently the singular nature of the issue had not been addressed previously. Although I had all the help I needed from agents in the Bangor office and elsewhere, it came down to this fact: I, as the case agent, had to make a potential life-or-death decision on the issue.

I had been discussing it with Assistant U.S. Attorney James McCarthy in Bangor. Together, we managed to defuse the situation by arresting three people on unrelated charges. A few weeks later, written policy from FBI headquarters supported the position I had taken. But the case took its toll on me mentally; I was near exhaustion. My squinting increased and I was having trouble concentrating again.

The summer of 1997 rolled along and my condition improved somewhat, although I still experienced constant heavy-headedness. I should have consulted a doctor, but I just didn't.

In late June or early July of 1997, I had occasion to return some documents to the Penobscot Indian Nation in Old Town, Maine. There I spoke with a senior manager, a Penobscot Indian who was a friend of mine. He told me: "Don, I'm surprised they haven't gotten you yet! There is not enough money in the world for me to do what you do."

Somewhat taken aback, I asked him: "Do you have any specific information concerning someone who plans to get me?" He said he didn't, so I asked him to let me know if he learned anything about such a threat, which had to do with several Native American issues I was looking at. He said he would, and I became very vigilant.

Two years earlier, I had received an anonymous letter at home, probably from a Native American who was trying to intimidate me. The contents were typed and the address on the envelope was hand-written.

It contained a poem titled "Never Trust An Indian." It had been mailed two days earlier after Cliv Dore, the tribal governor who fired Fred during the tobacco smuggling undercover operation, met with the tribe's attorney who was also the president and attorney for the Passamaquoddy Technology project that had lost millions of dollars. I think it had a Portland postmark.

Construction, research and development of the Passamaquoddy scrubber cost about $15 million. Most of it, about $13 million, came from government loans and grants, primarily from the Department of Energy and the Bureau of Indian Affairs. The scrubber was never commercially functional and it sits like a white elephant at the Dragon Cement Plant in Thomaston, Maine.

I had an unpublished telephone number, so whoever sent me that poem had to do some probing to get my address. I forwarded it to the Boston Division Evidence Room for safekeeping.

A few days after getting the verbal warning from the Penobscot, I was alone in the house taking a nap when an elastic band holding our sheets secure snapped off its corner. I heard the sharp crack/twang in my semi-dormant condition, immediately rolled out of bed, and lay prone. The noise had triggered a Vietnam combat reaction. It sounded like the crack of an incoming AK-47 round and I reacted instinctively. For the briefest moment, I was back in 'Nam. (At that time, by the way, I did not connect my combat experience to my continuing "heavy-headedness.")

By the end of July and early August 1997, I was beginning to feel better, although I still had head pressure and difficulty concentrating. Then In the middle of September, I got word that former Special Agent Livio "Al" Beccaccio had died in a fiery helicopter crash in Bosnia, where he was training the locals in police work. The news shook me up because two years earlier, Al had been transferred to the Bangor office waiting for retirement.

He had headed the FBI Academy's physical fitness program for several years and was also the head of the National FBI Academy for police officers. I was honored to serve with him at the street level in Bangor. During his short stay in Bangor, we solved a bank robbery, which filled him with pride. He told me, "I came into the Bureau working bank robberies and I'm leaving the Bureau working bank robberies."

The way he died depressed me deeply. I began to compare what he must have felt to the feelings I had when the CH-53 helicopter I was in lost power in Vietnam in September 1967.

All these events were beginning to take a toll. After Al's death, my concentration problems increased dramatically. At times, I had trouble understanding what people were saying to me. But I figured time and rest would take care of things. I told myself I would fight it.

But by September 1997, I was entering a different realm of mental illness and didn't realize it until several months later. My Bureau report writing was getting pompous and I was beginning to view myself as a conqueror of all evils in a sense, which was completely contradictory to my character. I didn't realize it then, but I know now that it was the beginning of the delusions of grandeur that surfaced five months later. And to make matters worse, delusions of persecution were emerging as well.

From September through January 1998, I tried to concentrate on three particularly important matters. One was being handled out of the Interior Department's office in Alexandria, Virginia, by Senior Special Agent Chuck Gifford. It involved allegations of fraud against the Bureau of Indian Affairs and payoffs to tribal leaders of the Passamaquoddy Tribe, both Indian Township and Pleasant Point reservations, in relation to the Passamaquoddy Technology project. Heavy-duty political names, not criminally associated, had surfaced during the investigation, which involved many interviews of Native Americans.

The second investigation concerned allegations of bribery against Native American public officials in relationship to a casino project. The casino was never built, but the allegations concerned payoffs made to Passamaquoddy leaders. Due to the sensitive nature of the investigation, I can't say much more than that. The investigation ended without anyone being charged or prosecuted, partly as a result of my developing mental problems. That matter was worked out of the Boston office, as the main players lived in the Boston and New York City areas.

I also got wrapped up in another Native American investigation of a potential criminal nature (again, I can't go into details because the people who cooperated were granted confidentiality), which was handled by the New York office of the FBI because some major players lived and worked in that area.

From September through January 1998, I helped out, traveling to Virginia, Boston and New York to pursue leads and meet with case agents, make decisions, etc. Several agents had been assigned to the investigations, and that alleviated much of the pressure on any one of us. But my plate was full.

By November 1997, I needed a break. So I took a week off and went deer hunting with my brothers-in-law, Randy and Don "Skip" Nelson, at The Forks in northwestern Maine. At the end of the week, I was in pretty good physical shape. Mentally, I felt I was starting to get sharp again.

Every night on that trip, I downed a few Buds and one or two shots of Jim Beam (I drank liquor only on extended trips once or twice a year) and felt like my old self. But it wasn't all relaxing. Early in the hunt, at the crossroads of two trails, a hunter shot at a buck and missed, but the bullet went right over my head and hit a few feet away. I jumped behind a tree and hollered, "Hey!" The hunter apologized, of course, but there it was again -- that Vietnam trigger.

The next Monday, after I returned to work, a friend of mine in the Bureau told me that Boston was keeping an eye on me. Apparently, they figured I was having a problem. I wondered where it would lead. Would they place my family and I under surveillance like they had back in August 1992, or what?

Paranoia consumed me. I hoped that if the Bureau had a reason to keep an eye on me, someone would approach me to discuss it. I learned later that they picked up on me as having problems in September. What attracted their attention was my written work. I never got all the details, but it was probably my pompous attitude showing itself in my writing.

In late November, I got word that federal prosecutors in Virginia had decided not to prosecute the Passamaquoddy Technology case, the one involving allegations of bribery of some former tribal chiefs and fraud against the Bureau of Indian Affairs. It concerned the smokestack scrubber technology that would remove solid precipitates from smokestack emissions. Several millions of dollars had been dumped into the project. It appeared that the attorney handling the defense of "P-Tech," as it was called, had intimidated the assistant U.S. attorney handling the case.

When we visited that prosecutor in September of 1997, he told Chuck Gifford and I that the defense attorney for Passamaquoddy Technology had come to his office and sat in a particular chair. He described this attorney, whose name I don't remember, as very high profile in Washington circles. What I'll never forget is that he got out of his chair repeatedly and pointed at the chair that the attorney had sat in, and said, "He sat right there, right there." I suspected then that the P-Tech case was lost.

By December, still involved in the Boston and New York matters, I was waiting for Boston management to approach me. Around that time, I happened to come face to face with Jay P. McCloskey, the U.S. Attorney for Maine, in his Bangor office. He glared at me and I saw hatred in his eyes. He did not like me one bit, as I didn't succumb to his control.

McCloskey took a positive attitude towards some investigations, but I personally believe he may have been upset as I transferred the Passamaquoddy Technology case to Virginia, which means he lost control of the matter.

That Christmas, my 24-year-old son Keith gave me a Christmas present. It was a framed print by artist Lee Teeter, and it showed the sad figures of five male soldiers and a female soldier looking out from the wall of the Vietnam Veterans Memorial. They're all gazing at a man wearing a suit and carrying a briefcase who had placed his right hand on the wall. His head was bowed in grief and memory. It occurred to me that he was probably also reflecting on his own survival in Vietnam.

I looked at the print and saw myself as the lone living figure in the picture, wondering why I survived. And the doleful expression on the suited man's face reminded me of the promise I had made to God on Sept. 5, 1967, to dedicate my life to the betterment of mankind. But I had failed, starting with the failure to take better care of myself as my drinking increased from three to four beers an evening to six to eight and at times 12 when I couldn't sleep at night. What's more, with a deepening mental illness exacerbated by the memories of Vietnam, I was not performing at my best.

With the failure of P-Tech and other cases to come, I truly was the man standing in that picture. As a law enforcement officer, I hadn't been tough enough, feeling responsible for the wasted P-Tech effort. But looking back on those days, I know there were other places to lay the blame. Of course, I wasn't in a state of good mental health at the time. I had let my Vietnam heroes down -- Vernon Randolph, Father Capodanno, Roland Guerette, Schmitty and all the others I knew who lost their lives over there.

One evening, I was by myself at home, gazing at that print and drinking a beer. Feeling heavy-hearted, I went to the record player, found a Bob Dylan record and played his version of Ira Hayes songs, had a few beers and sang along to "Not the Whiskey Drinking Indian" or "The Marine Who Went To War."

Right then, I felt it was just about over for me. The only thing keeping me going was pride and the overwhelming desire to protect my family from Bureau intrusion into our lives. Plus, I fretted constantly about those who might seek to harm me or harm my family. I told myself I'd fight this to the very last.

A few weeks earlier, I had learned that someone under investigation in the probe of the 1997 casino project involving some elements of the Genovese and Gambino crime families from New York had said, "Anyone who stands in my way, I will have beheaded." Beheaded? That brought back memories.

In January or February of 1998, things got worse. I had a flashback of the little boy who had been beheaded by the bombing in Vietnam in February 1967. His whole family had been killed. Somehow, in my warped thinking, this little boy represented my family and the "beheaded" comment by the Mafia guy was clearly directed at me. Now I figured I had to be on the lookout for the good guys as well as the bad guys. I was losing my sense of logic and reality.

Around that time, I went to the New York office to meet with the case agent on a matter I can't discuss because it's still too sensitive for public exposure. Special Agent Angelo Rinchuiso accompanied me from Boston. During the drive to New York City, I talked unceasingly about the case at hand and other Bangor issues. Every time he spoke, I squinted. Concentration on his words was next to impossible. I felt I had to dominate the conversation.

The following day, I made my presentation to the New York office case agent and the Assistant U.S. Attorney handling the matter. I don't recall if I did a good job, made a fool of myself, or what. All I do remember is thinking and speaking very rapidly.

Looking back on it, I was suffering from delusions of grandeur and some form of mania. It was strange. I knew I was having problems, but somehow I still considered myself sane and rational. I kept denying the obvious.

I don't recall much else about January and February of 1998. A few months earlier I had picked up on drinking beer and that became my sleeping sedative. Now I was no longer drinking because I enjoyed it. Now I needed the alcohol to fall asleep at night.

My wife and children were becoming quite concerned about the beer drinking. I didn't say much on the subject, but did admit to my son Keith that I was having a drinking problem. Donna told me later that she was worried because she detected some deterioration in my thinking. We never really discussed it, though.

I was fighting an insidious enemy as I had more and more trouble sleeping. I was working 10-12 hours a day, which is pretty standard in the Bureau, and then getting three or four hours of sleep a night. In mid-February, I decided I had some serious mental problems as well as alcohol abuse. I intended to tell management about it when the Boston supervisor, Bruce Ellavsky, and the Assistant Special Agent in Charge, Richard Watson, visited the Bangor office in late February. They were good guys, and I think at least part of the reason for their visit was to check up on me.

The morning I was to meet with them, I sat in my chair, crossed myself and said the "Our Father." I had had enough. I couldn't go on in the condition I was in. I suspected that my superiors were there to relieve me of my duties, or possibly even to arrest me for unknown crimes. Delusions of persecution had rooted themselves in my mind. I was truly ill and becoming incoherent.

W.H., one of my partners in the Bangor office, entered the office first and I couldn't speak to him. I was pretty well choked up. Ellavsky and Watson followed. W.H. told them there was something wrong with me. I asked to meet with them in the interview room, which we did. I was prepared to brief them on my condition and I planned to ask to go on sick leave until I could straighten myself out.

But the meeting turned into a major breakdown. I had so much pent-up conflicting emotions that I recall saying something anguished like "Aaah! Aaah!" Then I began to weep, telling them about my concerns and the safety of my family.

They could see that I was truly ill. They asked me for my Sig Sauer Model 23, which I unloaded, cleared and handed over. So it was out. I felt some relief, fear for the future and for my family, and lingering anxiety. My life as I had known it for 50 years had come to an abrupt halt.

The supervisor and Assistant Special Agent in Charge appeared to be quite concerned about my condition. The supervisor would tell me later that he never realized how much I had been suffering. He called my wife at the Bangor nursing home where she worked and she gave me a ride home. After I left the interview room, I sat in my chair for the last time. W.H. and Paul Palumbo, my other partner in the Bangor office, both had tears in their eyes.

Once at home, I resolved to stop drinking and cope with my sleep problems as best I could. I was to go to Boston the following day for an interview about my breakdown, but my condition worsened, and insomnia wrenched from me the rest of my sanity. I lay awake for six or seven nights and days, which included the trip to Boston, without any sleep relief.

Meanwhile, of course, Donna and the kids were getting very worried. They did their best to comfort me without really knowing what was going on.

Slowly, I entered the world of the insane, the psychotic. It got to the point where I was hearing messages from the fireplace at home, talking directly to the director of the FBI through the fireplace, believing that the Bureau had placed a bug in the fireplace. I was in bad, bad shape -- delusional and sliding in and out of reality.

One condition I experienced shortly after my breakdown was excessive scrupulousness. Looking back, I reflected on 27 years of government service, examining every facet of my employment, and essentially came up with nothing really derogatory. In 27 years I had missed work only two days very early in my career because of excessive alcohol consumption.

I also examined my spiritual life and was appalled at my sinfulness. Spiritual re-examination, remorse and forgiveness would come at a later date.

The following day, after my breakdown and with no sleep at all, my wife and I went to Boston, with Paul driving, for a couple days of interviews with two agents from Boston who handle the Employee Assistance Program (EAP). Donna and I stayed at a hotel in Boston. I was in and out of reality. At any given time, I might be logical and rational, and at others, I'd go off the deep end.

For example, early on the morning of our second day in Boston, Donna was in the bathroom. Although the room we stayed in was a non-smoking room, I lit up a Marlboro. In what must have been a pathetic show of defiance, I bowed to what I perceived to be the north, smoked a puff, and did the same to the east, south and west.

I suppose smoking tobacco was as "sacred" as things could get, sacred in the sense that Roland Guerette had given me my first smoke in Vietnam, and he was killed, and smoking was a reminder of his death. I also thought to myself, "Damn, why did he (Al Beccaccio) have to die the way he did?"

Then I thought to myself, "The hell with the Mohawk Warrior Society," and put out the cigarette. They had brought sacred tobacco into the federal courthouse during the trial and sprinkled it all over the floor.

Later that morning, I met with the EAP agents, who showed me a lot of compassion. I don't recall too much about the conversations we had, but I do know that I was told I would be flown to Washington,

D.C., for a psychological evaluation. I would return to Bangor on Thursday or Friday, and on Monday, I would fly to Washington.

But my son Keith, who was working in a hospital at the time as a medical student, vehemently opposed the Bureau, telling them I was very sick. They got the point and scheduled a psychologist to come up to Boston and interview me the following week.

During that time, my daughters Kristen, 21, who was a student at the University of Southern Maine, and Karen, 26, who was working in Connecticut as a drug rehabilitation therapist, were both at home caring for me. After Donna and I returned from Boston, I spent a few more sleepless nights at the house awaiting the psychologist's arrival in Boston.

In early March, Paul drove Keith and I to Boston. On the trip, while still in Maine, I imagined that all my old friends and acquaintances were lining I-95 in their tractor-trailer rigs and cars watching me leave the state. That was the state of my delusions.

In Boston, the psychologist gave me a written test. After answering the first 25 percent or so of the questions, I figured this was child's play. Of course I loved my mother and father! At one point, I got angry and ripped up the test.

The doctor was pretty upset, according to my son, and rightly so. About an hour later, he interviewed me. I don't recall how long it lasted or what we said. Everything remained a blank.

I still was not sleeping at all and after Keith left and I went to bed, I snuck out of the hotel room, meandered around town for a while, sat on a bench and had a smoke. Then, according to Keith, I began to walk around town doing the German goose step, and people gave me a wide berth. After he told me about it, I remember doing the goose step, but I have no idea why.

My son ended up walking the streets looking for me. He found me and we returned to the hotel room. To my surprise, Keith was angry with me. I tried to get some sleep, but again to no avail, while my son lay in front of the hotel room door barring any future "escapes."

The following day I went in for an interview with the Assistant Special Agent in Charge, Richard Watson, and others. Someone asked if I would check myself into Massachusetts General Hospital. I agreed because I knew I needed help desperately.

Agent Watson drove us to the hospital. Before checking in, the psychologist, Keith and an EAP special agent and I sat in the waiting room. Sitting opposite from us was a patient with his leg in a cast and his left arm in a sling.

"Lo and behold," I thought. It was Uncle Phil from Connecticut. I thought he'd died a few years earlier. I walked over to him, introduced myself, spoke to him briefly, and then returned to my seat. It was not, of course, Uncle Phil. It was another delusion.

We were called into the admitting office, and I signed in. I was pretty proud of myself. Six or seven days of sleeplessness and I could still write my name legibly. From there, we all went to the psychiatric unit and said our good-byes. At one point, I spotted two female patients who I thought were my daughters.

Someone took me to the isolation ward, where I was assigned a room furnished with a dresser and a hospital bed with an air mattress. In retrospect, I know I was placed on a suicide watch because they took away my belt and razor and checked to make certain I had swallowed my sleeping and anti-psychotic meds. While waiting to be examined by a psychiatrist, I saw a Hispanic male who I thought was my bodyguard walk by the door, doing his karate thing. Everyone else, I thought, were imposters.

Early that evening, I was taken into a white padded cell that contained a single restraint jacket. I didn't see any chairs in the room and I was terrified that I would be locked up. I sat in a heap on the floor while a male psychiatrist in his late 30s to early 40s interviewed me. I don't recall much except mumbling something about losing a lot of friends in Vietnam. I did express deep remorse for my father's heart attack after I was wounded the second time in Vietnam. Everything else was a blur. And I recall that at the end of the interview, the psychiatrist was misty-eyed.

I returned to my room and nurses checked on me throughout the night. I was feisty and argumentative one moment and polite the next. I refused blood work and other testing. I didn't sleep at all that night even though I was sedated. During the next couple days I did agree to blood testing and a CAT scan of my brain. The blood work came back negative and the CAT scan showed a degree of aging, nothing unusual.

I was still plagued by "heavy-headedness" and a constant brain buzz. The buzz manifested itself when I had my breakdown back in the FBI office in Bangor. It took weeks to subside.

While in the psychiatric unit, I did some pretty crazy things. That first evening, someone gave me a menu for the following day. It was divided into three sections -- breakfast, lunch and dinner, with several choices for each section. I completely misunderstood the form. Thinking it was a psychological test, I checked every single item in each section. How could I go wrong? The next morning, they gave me bacon and eggs.

I had an airbed. Every time I lay down on it, it let out a mild whooshing sound. When I got up, it made a similar reverse sort of sound. The mattress became my judge and jury. If I had good thoughts, I got out of bed. The whooshing sound happened and I thought to myself, "These thoughts are no good." Then I'd lie back in bed and the reverse sound confirmed my latest thinking. It was wild. I kept getting in and out of bed. Whoever was monitoring me must have thought I was nuts!

Another problem was the television set. When I turned it on during the first few days of my stay, messages on behavior beamed out at me, no matter what I watched. When the news was on, I found myself commiserating with everyone in the news in some strange form. I don't recall much else. Everyone's story seemed so distorted. It took me several days to realize that those were delusions, too.

On the third or fourth day there, I asked to see a Catholic priest. One evening he came in to visit me. I made a full confession and received absolution. He gave me a set of rosary beads, blessed me and wished me well. I briefly thought he was an imposter, but when I looked at the beads and said prayers, I realized that he was legit.

About the same time, the staff allowed me to mix occasionally with the general population of patients. I talked some to one in particular who wore a black leather jacket like my daughter Karen wore. Early on, I thought she was in fact my daughter when I saw her through the window of the isolation area.

Once out there, I sat back and sipped some ginger ale and looked around. I noticed that when doctors or nurses punched a few numbers on a security pad, the door to the floor opened and they left. Just out of idle curiosity, I decided to leave the ward by following closely the next person to exit. Sure enough, within minutes, some staff members punched the security code in, the door opened and they left with me right on their tail.

That caused a near panic as someone on the staff spotted me heading out. I was quickly apprehended and returned to isolation for a couple more days. That made me very lonely for home. So being delusional, I devised an escape plan. When the time was right, I planned to leave the ward, walk outside and get a ride or walk back home.

A couple days went by before I was released once again into the general population. I made two phone calls, one to the Boston office of the FBI requesting that they come down and arrest me for drug dealing. Again, there was no rhyme or reason to what was going through my head.

The other call was to my son Keith, to tell him about my escape plan. He told me I was crazy and he wouldn't help me. Needless to say, he probably notified the Bureau or the medical staff of my plans. Back into isolation I went, losing my roaming privileges.

One evening, a female patient was admitted into the isolation part of the ward. As they wheeled her in, I noticed that her eyes were hazel in color, which made me think she was my wife. I entered the room with the staff, walked to the foot of her bed and just stared at her until staff members rushed me out of the room.

Fortunately for what peace of mind I could muster, Donna, who drove from her parents' home in Lewiston to Boston on an almost daily basis (her employer had given her the time she needed to be with me, and we still lived in Bangor), brought me a cassette tape called "Oceans." I listened to it for hours at a time, drifting off into my own tranquil world.

After several days of treatment with various drugs (I have no recollection what drugs they gave me), my condition was not improving. Donna and my daughter Kristen complained to the staff, and they finally gave me the anti-psychotic drug Trilafon, administered as a pill, initially at 64 mg, later dropped to 32 mg. That did the trick.

In a day or two, I finally exited the world of the psychotic, and my paranoia disappeared for several months. One nurse called it a "miracle drug." I would be on it for some four years in decreasing doses, ending up at 2 mg a day.

The sleeping medication they gave me was also working. I was getting eight hours of sleep a night. My recovery was quick, but not complete. While the head pressure and buzzing were abating, it would take many months, almost a year, to recover fully.

After being on Trilafon therapy for several days, I was transferred to the general ward area and assigned a room with another patient. I was also allowed to leave the hospital and travel around Boston.

Fifteen days into my stay at Mass. General, they let me go, but not before a psychiatrist explained that as a condition of my release, I had to agree to take my medications daily, join an AA group and get a private psychiatrist. I insisted on a psychiatrist in southern Maine as there were too many "eyes and ears" in the Bangor area.

Together, a hospital counselor and I found a great one, Dr. Jerome Collins, who worked out of Kennebunk, Maine. But he couldn't see me for several weeks, so they gave me a two-month supply of Trilafon.

In May 1998, Donna and I walked into Dr. Collins' office to start what became a wonderful and rewarding relationship. He had served in the Army as a psychiatrist, was a former professor of psychiatry at Harvard University, and had decades of experience.

The first session lasted an hour after our introductions, and I tried to explain what I had suffered the past several months. He told me that sleep deprivation appeared to be my biggest problem. In a recent study in England, he said scores of students were sleep-deprived. After three or four days of that, every last one of the students developed a psychosis.

Dr. Collins also told me that I had suffered a neuro-transmission problem, and that dopamine, a neurotransmitter that we all produce naturally in our brains, was out of whack. Trilafon regulated the culprit. That meant my problems had been organic in nature, exacerbated by stress, loss of sleep and alcohol consumption. Why else would the Trilafon work? Simple deductive reasoning.

CHAPTER 11

FALL INTO PERDITION
AND A GLIMPSE OF HEAVEN

St. Jude was the brother of St. Simon the Zealot. He was known as the Big-Hearted. In the year 0067, he was clubbed to death for his belief in Christ Jesus. He died for the Greater Glory of God.

About four weeks before meeting Dr. Collins, and shortly after leaving Massachusetts General Hospital, I ran into a new challenge -- religion. I was recovering nicely at home, and one day I was resting on our bed when I fell unexpectedly into a state of deep despair and depression. My immediate reaction was to pray earnestly to Our Lord and ask Him the following questions: Why did this happen to me? How was I to recover and regain my self-esteem, respect and reputation with the Bureau and with my friends and family?

I had been a solid employee, a good worker, a good father and a good parent, and my motives were always above reproach. Additionally, I had devoted my life's work to the service of God. I lay there helpless as my despair deepened and I felt myself falling into the dark abyss of Perdition. I was descending into Hell. All was black. Absolute fear. A black hole of complete despair.

Suddenly, the hand of a loving Father stopped my fall. There I was, falling into a black hole of despair and I recall a hand gently swooping under me and bringing me, my soul, back up. I was brought back from the edge of the cliff. It was no delusion. I am convinced that it was real.

Just like that, my questions had answers. It happened because of my "human condition." I would recover if I "acted naturally," being myself. In a way, I was admonished, a reminder that I was one of those targeted in the age-old phrase, "Ye of so little faith."

A few days later, I was lying in bed resting once again, home alone. I was praying to Father Capodanno, to my father and mother and all those who departed before me. Without warning, I experienced a phenomenon I had never felt before and probably will not know again until my death. I was transported into a realm of extreme ecstasy.

This place was devoid of color, time, space or any type of dimension. I entered a world where pain and suffering no longer existed. A world of complete love that words cannot fully explain. I was completely content, joyous and peaceful. I was in the presence of a power of untold magnificence, a state of complete ecstasy, for about four hours.

When I arose, I was awestruck. I had been given a glimpse of heaven. Some may describe what happened as a form of mania, but no one can ever refute or fully explain what I experienced that afternoon. It was no delusion, but was in fact real.

I had drifted away from the church, defiant of God despite my many blessings. Over the next year, I gradually returned to my Catholic roots. In doing so, I am convinced that Satan plagued me. The closer I came to God, the more intense the efforts to alienate me from Him. I was constantly and relentlessly being reminded of my past sins and the pleasures I had taken in committing them.

I bought several books -- the "Catholic Catechism" (a look at the contemporary catechism from the perspective of a Jesuit priest, Father Hardon); "Apparitions, Mystic Phenomena and What They Mean" by Kevin Orlin Johnson, Ph.D.; "The Case for Christ" by Lee Strobel, and others. I also bought a new Catholic Bible and a contemporary Catholic Catechism.

I began to piece together the roots of my beliefs. I learned from Father Hardon's book that "the devil is never permitted to tempt us beyond our strength." Those who do evil in the world are responsible for their own choices, as God gives everyone the ability to use free will. If someone resists temptation, that temptation will not be beyond his or her strength to resist. In other words, the Devil plants an idea in the head of an individual, who is then free to follow the Devil's lead or resist.

Satan is the "consummate deceiver." He is Satan because he is an "adversary" who plots against you, I or anyone on this earth. "He is a demon because he is a spiritual being possessed of extraordinary powers," according to Father Hardon. The devil is a "calumniator" who accuses those he has deceived of the sins that they have committed.

Bingo!

Voraciously, I read everything I could get my hands on about the Catholic faith. To ensure complete recovery, renewal of my Catholicism was as vital to me as the anti-psychotic and anti-depressant medication I was taking. I learned that you cannot separate the psyche (mind) from the soul. They are inexorably intertwined, symbiotic to one another.

During my recovery on sick and administrative leave, we lived in a house we owned in Brewer, Maine. I attended Mass regularly. At times, I found a distortion in the music being sung, which I attributed to devilish delusion, while finding great joy and solace in songs such as "The Prayer of St. Francis:" "O Lord, let me be the instrument of thy peace. Where there is hatred let me sow love..."

I know those distortions represented an evil presence in my life. During my breakdown, Satan probably saw an opening into my soul and exploited it to its fullest. Along the way, I occasionally had abnormal thoughts about sexual matters. They were unwanted thoughts about filth I had known of in my life, absolutely without participating in any such acts.

For example, when I was stationed in California at Camp Pendleton, I heard about a prostitute who went on stage and pretended to have sex with a donkey. I never went to see that, but I was being plagued by the vision. It's true -- the devil *is* a "calumniator!"

As I recovered from my mental illness, I continued to devour those religious books, including the Bible. It pleased me to see that the Catholic doctrines I had been brought up under had not changed appreciably. Some church laws had been softened, such as abstaining from eating meat on Friday, but there was nothing really significant.

I thought of and prayed to Father Capodanno and Vernon Randolph, the heroic priest and heroic Marine, almost daily. I adopted a prayer that I recited every day, "Father, please forgive me of all my sins, have mercy on my soul, and bring me to everlasting life."

Going through that ecstasy still affects me profoundly. I do not fear death. I will welcome it when my time on earth is through, for I know that Heaven is real and I will strive to attain it.

In my readings, I also learned several things. One is the difference between Catholicism and other Christian denominations. Catholic teachings originate in and are affected by doctrinal theology and mystic theology, whereas other denominations are guided by doctrinal theology alone. Mystic theology refers to a study of mystical phenomena such as levitations, appearances by Holy Figures, stigmata (the wounded hands of Christ manifested in a few individuals such as Padre Pio), visions, ecstasies, tears of joy and other phenomena. (A more detailed description is available in the book "Apparitions and Mystic Phenomena," by Kevin Orlin Johnson, PhD.)

Also, Catholics believe in the primacy of the Pope and his linear succession from St. Peter through the ages. Most non-Catholics do not accept this fundamental truth. It may be that accepting the Pope that way would challenge their sense of autonomy.

I also learned that non-Catholics and people of various faiths throughout the world can be saved without becoming Catholic -- as long as they sincerely seek God and abide by moral law and the Ten Commandments. I believe those who have been taught the Ten Commandments should follow them as best as they can. Those who have no idea and no commonly known faiths can also reach heaven if they truly try to identify God and live as morally as they can.

I have always believed in the life, death and resurrection of Jesus Christ. My intensive readings and the ecstasy I experienced confirmed that faith. The death of Father Capodanno -- who uttered to the dying Marines on the battlefield, "Christ is the truth and the life" -- also buttressed my belief. He died for the faith, was martyred and is now being considered for beatification. His death was the ultimate sacrifice for our God and his teachings through Our Lord Jesus Christ. His death humbled me and reaffirmed my Catholic teachings.

In the year 2000, I had the distinct pleasure of speaking on the phone with Tom Forgas, who was present when Father Capodanno was killed 33 years earlier. He said his life was affected deeply by the Padre's death, as was mine. I also spoke extensively with Jim Hamfeldt, and each time we remembered the priest with great fondness.

In 1990, while I was assigned to the New York office of the FBI, Jim gave me the location of Father Capodanno's gravesite in Staten Island. On a Sunday afternoon, I took Donna and the kids to the cemetery, where we visited with Father Cap and said prayers over his remains. I recalled that fateful day, Sept. 4, 1967, when he died in the service of his Marines. I found myself asking, not for the first time, about the meaning of death.

CHAPTER 12

THE ROAD TO RECOVERY AND RETURN TO WORK

St. James the Greater, the larger brother of St. James the Less, was the first of the apostles to die. He was beheaded in the year 0042 and is the patron saint of Spain. He died for the Greater Glory of God.

Analyzing my circumstances in the spring of 1998, I realized my recovery depended on five distinct challenges. I would have to:

- Resolve my differences with Our Lord.
- Abstain from drinking alcohol and attend Alcoholics Anonymous as directed by the FBI.
- Take my medication religiously and see Dr. Collins regularly.
- Determine my future with the FBI.
- Undergo intensive psychological examination by a Bureau-appointed psychiatrist and psychologist. I had to emotionally survive the inquest that was sure to follow.

Alcohol wasn't really a problem. Over the years, I was always able to stop drinking without any negative effects such as delirious tremens. Nor was joining AA. The organization exists solely to aid the recovering alcoholic, and I attended once a week for two years. Oddly enough, I found myself doubting my opening statement at every meeting: "Hi, I'm Don. I'm an alcoholic." I frankly didn't know if that was true. Nevertheless, I attended as a condition of continued employment.

One issue that surfaced immediately with AA was the nature of my problems. I couldn't talk to anyone about my work as an FBI agent, and two separate sponsors (the people at AA who take you under their wing) told me not to identify myself as a law enforcement officer because some AA members hated authority figures.

Also of concern was hearing the "confessions" of other members. Some admitted to committing crimes, and other talked about various other depredations. That put me in a precarious position as a law enforcement officer. You might think that what you say at an AA meeting is kept confidential, but some time ago, a member in another state declared that he had murdered someone and provided details. Several members of the AA group told the police, and then a court fight ensued. The court upheld the confidentiality of the AA meeting, but an appellate court reversed the decision, and the defendant was convicted.

Then there was religion. The AA's 12-step program is based on religious precepts. The first step is to acknowledge that you are powerless over alcohol and that there is a higher power in the world above the self. That power can be a living tree, the firmament, a mountain or a light bulb.

AA vigorously denies that it is a religious organization. Otherwise, many would not join. Many AA members reject authority. Telling members they can use an inanimate object as their higher power seems misguided to me. This is not necessarily AA doctrine, but it is the approach AA takes towards bringing someone to accept a higher authority.

The key here is that an alcoholic must humble himself or herself before a higher power. To my way of thinking, that step is contrary to the First Commandment, which says: "I am the Lord your God. You shall have no other Gods before me. You shall not make for yourself a graven image, or any likeness of anything that is in heaven above or that is in the earth beneath, or that is in the water under the earth. You shall not bow down to them or serve them. It is written that you shall worship the Lord your God and him only shall you serve."

When you have someone encouraging another that it's okay to worship a tree or a light bulb that goes contrary to the 1st Commandment. The thinking in AA is that once you believe in a higher power, it can be elevated from an inanimate object to an animated one up to God Himself.

Yet another issue is acknowledging your sins and any crimes you may have been involved in to your sponsor. The inherent problem here, from my view as a Catholic, is that the sponsor cannot give you absolution. Only a priest can do that. Of course, going through hell is the common experience of the alcoholic and a cessation of drinking is paramount to recovery. AA does an excellent job of bringing together those who have been beaten down by this dreaded disease, but it must be remembered that the recidivism rate is as high as with any other program.

Spiritual help and temporal help are hallmarks of the program. But still, the sponsor who you may confide in cannot give you absolution, which was necessary for my recovery. My sins are between my confessor, God and myself and no one else.

In 1999, the Seventh Circuit of the U.S. Court of Appeals ruled that Alcoholics Anonymous is a religion. Therefore, no one can be court-ordered or coerced by any government agency to attend. Involvement with AA should be a personal choice. That does, of course, create a problem for federal, state and local agencies and hospitals that use the AA program to assist employees, patients, prisoners and probationers.

Taking my medication was not a problem. Dr. Collins prescribed some very specific dosages to help me along and they had a generally positive effect. Under his care I initially took 32 mg of Trilafon daily and by the end of my career, I was taking 2 mg a day as I progressed.

But FBI headquarters, backed by Bureau doctors, said I could not return to full duty -- bearing a firearm, serving subpoenas, conducting arrests and searches -- until I was off the psychotic and sleeping medications. I was taking Ambien and Trazadone to help me sleep and to minimize the effects of depression, and I still take them.

During the first eight months of my treatment by Dr. Collins, I was down to 4 mg of Trilafon by December 1998. However, I began to get paranoid and my thinking started to deteriorate. I thought I was being followed and started to give undue significance to such mundane things as vanity plates. I realized it was happening after four to six weeks, and decided to do something about it.

Dr. Collins increased my Trilafon to 16 mg. I felt very comfortable at that level. I was logical and rational. Gradually, we reduced the Trilafon dosage to 8 mg when I returned to work in May 1999 on less than full duty. So I learned that the healing process for a neurological problem takes time. By the end of my career, I was down to 2 mg of Trilafon per day. Today, I'm completely off it.

After about a year and a half of caring for me, Dr. Collins said, "Don, your psychological problems stem from post-traumatic stress disorder." I had opened up to him about the various triggers that afflicted me in the winter of 1997-98, and how they related to combat situations in Vietnam.

That's when everything began to fall into place. What had been disconnected issues suddenly connected. It all made sense. Shortly thereafter, Dr. Collins, who was about to retire, referred me to a psychotherapist, a lady from the Kittery, Maine, area who I'd rather not identify.

And it worked out great. In an atmosphere lacking any pressure, unlike the Bureau interviews, I sat back, relaxed and discussed Vietnam memories and how they related to my work. I told her about the boy who was beheaded when they accidentally dropped that bomb. I talked about the deaths of Father Capodanno and Vernon Randolph, as well as that of Al Beccaccio.

We spoke of "triggers" I had encountered, such as the bad guy threatening, "I will behead anyone who steps in my way." We spoke of the elastic bed band incident and the way I reacted. We also discussed the Indian poem someone had sent to my home and how all those problems interacted with my psychotic state at the time.

Shortly thereafter, Dr. Collins had more news: I was not an alcoholic. That was a stunner, since I had told him about my daily use of beer, which increased in 1997 as work pressures built up. He dismissed that as adjusting to stresses of the job, and added that I used beer to self-medicate. With that, a burden of major proportions fell off my shoulders.

Another pressing problem was my demeanor toward the Bureau doctors during interviews in April and October 1998 and again in August 1999.

During the first interview, the doctor put me under intense pressure by asking questions rapidly, trying to assess my psychological condition. But, having been released from Mass. General only four or five weeks earlier, I was still reeling from the effects of the psychological trauma.

The Bureau doctors determined that the medications were causing just a partial remission of my afflictions at first. Recovery was a slow process. So they scheduled me for the October interview. They did the same testing -- both written and intensive interviewing -- and found me to be in full remission: no more psychotic symptoms, delusions of grandeur, delusions of persecution, paranoia and the like.

However, they did find that I had low stress tolerance and was predisposed to depression. I waited four months before their reports made it through the FBI bureaucracy. In February 1999, the Boston Assistant Special Agent in Charge, Richard Watson, drove to the Augusta, Maine, FBI office and met with Donna and I.

He was pleased to tell me that I was to be transferred in May to the Boston Division, where I would be a non-weapon bearing special agent, working applicant and national security background investigations. It would be a temporary position. What a relief. I was going back to work. The anxiety I'd been dealing with during the past year would soon abate.

In May 1999, Donna and I moved to Kittery, which is on the New Hampshire border in southern Maine. By then, our kids had struck out on their own, with Kristen graduating from the University of Southern Maine with a degree in communications, Keith graduating from the University of New England School of Medicine, and Karen getting a Master's degree in family counseling from the University of Connecticut. Kristen is now a senior insurance specialist with Unum Provident and Keith is a physician with a specialty in internal medicine in Pittsburgh. Keith recently won a fellowship in the field of critical care and has moved to Richmond, Virginia. And Karen owns a family counseling business with two friends in Connecticut.

While waiting for a mobile home we had bought to be delivered, we lived in a hotel for a month while I commuted daily to Boston, a round trip of 110 miles. (Donna was licensed as a CNA in Maine and we didn't want to leave the state.)

My first day at work, I met with Charles Prouty, the Special Agent in Charge in Boston. He welcomed me back and said he'd do everything he could to keep me onboard until my retirement date in February 2002. My intentions were always to return to full duty and put in my 20 years. Had the Bureau forced me to retire with a couple or three years left, I would have lost some pension funds. In any case, quitting just isn't my style.

Prouty said he had a close acquaintance, another Vietnam vet, who suffered from PTSD and related ailments. Assistant Special Agent in Charge Jim Burkett, and various supervisory special agents were also on my side. The supervisor of the applicant squad told me his priority was to see me through the next two years.

In late 2000, FBI headquarters in D.C. checked in to see whether to continue my limited duty status. At the time, I was down to 2 mg of Trilafon a day. I had had no recurrence of psychotic symptoms, which had abated completely by October 1998. I did regress a bit the following winter when it came to paranoia and depression, but we got that under control. FBI HQ allowed me to stay on limited duty status until retirement.

In Boston, I primarily did Special Inquiry Unit investigations on presidential appointees and interviewed prospective special agent candidates. The Bureau doctors said I had a low threshold for stress and depressive features. These would be tested by various investigations I was assigned because they carried with them specific timelines for completion, sometimes one or two days. What's more, you could have several investigations going on at the same time, some of which could be an appointee like the defense secretary or the treasury secretary. As it turned out, I handled the job without any problems.

Then came 9/11. My job that day was "daytime complaint agent," which meant fielding phone calls from the general public throughout New England. I also dealt with walk-ins who said they had information about the attacks, were seeking information, or filing actual complaints.

The calls I took showed how fear had gripped the region. Scores of callers volunteered their services to the FBI. Scores more were apprehensive and downright scared. Numerous businesses offered to help. Many fretted about the security of Boston's infrastructure -- utilities, public safety, hospitals and the like.

On the phone, I comforted many of them, mostly the elderly. The assignment required that I document all complaints, so I was extremely busy writing between calls. Eventually, the 10 or so days I spent on complaint duty passed quickly. I had done my job well with no ill effects.

Still, I suffered from depression to an extent. Early in the morning, I had a difficult time getting going, but once I took a shower, I was okay. By then, Dr. Collins had retired and referred me to a psychiatrist in Kennebunk, Maine, named Dr. David Jones, who treated me for depression with Zoloft. Later on, I began to see a Veterans Administration psychiatrist.

At the time, I was still in a sort of limbo with FBI headquarters in Washington. I knew that my return to work as a special agent was a temporary solution. I *didn't* know what the final outcome of my career would be, which added to my anxiety.

But through the grace of God and support from Prouty, Burkett and my immediate supervisor in Boston, as well as a Washington attorney I retained, I finished my career with dignity and honor. I retired on February 23, 2002, exactly 20 years and one day after I took my oath of office. At my retirement party, 70 to 75 people showed up, and I bid my adieu, thanking everyone for their support. That was the end of that. I had other problems to face.

Four days later, I had quadruple-bypass open-heart surgery at Portsmouth General Hospital in New Hampshire. I had detected a problem in September of the previous year -- shortness of breath when I exerted myself. And that was only the first of many physical afflictions I would suffer in the next few years.

CHAPTER 13

2002 - 2008

St. Bartholomew, an apostle of Christ, was skinned alive and beheaded for the Catholic faith in 0074. He died for the Greater Glory of God.

I assumed a low-key existence, savoring my retirement. Donna and I went to Popham Beach on the coast of Maine frequently. My children were bearing precious gifts of love -- their children. From 2002 until 2006, Donna and I became proud grandparents four times. How joyous it has been to bear witness to new life.

After my brief psychotic episode and subsequent transfer to Boston, I had only occasional contact with Fred Moore. We called occasionally to see what was going on in each other's lives. But I was a bit preoccupied with medical problems. The heart surgery I mentioned in the last chapter was only the beginning.

In 2004, at the VA Medical Center in Roxbury, Mass., I had carotid artery surgery on the right side of my neck. They cleared it out because it was 90 percent clogged from cholesterol buildup. And the next year a VA surgeon at St. Mary's Hospital in Lewiston, Maine, banded (that is, sealed) my bleeding esophageal varices (veins) that had been diagnosed several years earlier. I had had a bout of vomiting from eating clam linguine, which apparently caused the bleeding. Bleeding varices can be caused by excessive drinking. And I'm waiting for a VA vascular surgeon to decide if I need surgery on my left carotid artery, which is likely.

Then there's the diabetes, which can be traced to Agent Orange, the defoliant used widely by U.S. forces in Vietnam. It was diagnosed in 2004, and now I take glyburide twice a day to lower my blood sugars.

Doctors also blamed my medical problems on hereditary factors, excessive alcohol consumption and diet. For me, that meant more than six beers nightly in 1997 until I stopped drinking completely in 1998. I stayed off the alcohol until 2004, and now and then I have a few beers, nothing serious. Once in a great while when my wife and I go out, I'll have a glass of wine or one cocktail.

As far as food intake, I was raised on a diet that included daily egg consumption, greasy pork chops and other fatty meats that were common in the French-Canadian community of Lewiston in the '50s and early '60s.

In 2004, I increased my contacts with Fred. He told me that within two days of my breakdown in 1998, Passamaquoddy politicians had heard of my "craziness." The breakdown was supposed to be known only to my family, the FBI and the U.S. Attorney's Office in Bangor. But apparently, word had leaked out to people I had investigated over the years.

Using one of Fred's favorite sayings, "Oh well, life goes on," we moved forward. Fred continued as the Passamaquoddy Tribe's representative to the Maine State Legislature. He had served from 1994 until 1998 and was elected again in 2002 to serve until 2006.

After we re-established our relationship in 2004, we put out feelers for local writers who would like to help with "Chesuncook." There were no takers. It looked like we'd have to do it ourselves.

In August 2005, Donna and I attended the annual Franco–American Festival at Railroad Park in Lewiston, Maine, our new home where we had moved to be near with our loved ones. It's always a good time, and features French Canadian food and entertainers. In one tent, we found a ten-year-old girl from Fort Kent, Maine, named Melanie Saucier. She was singing French and Acadian songs.

We listened to her sing the French song that starts, "Quand le soleil dit bonjour aux montagnes, et que la nuit rencontre le jour, je suis seule avec mes reves sur la montagne, je ne veux penser qu'a toi." Translated, it goes something like, "When the sun greets the mountain in the morning and the dawn meets the day, I am alone with my dreams on the mountain. I don't want to think of anyone but you."

It was my mother's favorite song and she played it regularly on a record player at home after Dad passed away. Hearing it in that tent that August day reminded me of the love Donna and I shared on Sabattus Mountain and of our love for Mom and Dad. I decided then and there that Melanie Saucier's rendition would find a place in "Chesuncook."

Two months earlier, I was reading a column written by crime reporter Mark LaFlamme in the Lewiston Sun Journal. His imagination, his command of the English language and his take on life in general impressed me. I still had not made the commitment to write. But I did reach out to him. What I didn't know was that Mark had won awards for his column, and that he was writing a horror thriller titled "The Pink Room."

My initial contacts with him were congenial but guarded discussions. Slowly, I briefed him on the project Fred and I were thinking of taking on. He liked it, and I emailed him frequently for advice. All along, I had qualms about announcing my mental illness to the world, but Mark encouraged me to forge ahead, to be "assertive and bold." He also provided practical advice on hang-ups such as writers block. He said it was a common problem, and told me not to lose interest in writing if I had something worth saying.

In the summer of 2006, three events spurred me to forge ahead. In June, while rereading the U.S. Government-vs.-Francis Boots matter on the Internet, I discovered that the U.S. Supreme Court had ruled in the Pasquantino matter.

That same month, I learned that Father Vincent Capodanno had been selected by the Catholic Church for canonization. He had been given the official title "Servant of God." Now I really did feel compelled to write "Chesuncook." There were just too many timely coincidences coming together within a year.

Another motivator was an article in the VFW magazine that Jim Hamfeldt mailed to me. It described the deadliest battles fought in Vietnam. Operation Swift was featured under the title "Deadly Day at Dong Son." How well I remembered.

Were these three developments coincidental, or something else? I'm not sure, but that's when I committed myself to "Chesuncook."

As I was getting started, Fred told me he was going to run for tribal governor in the Passamaquoddy election in September 2006. That brought back memories of my time with the Native Americans, so I decided to attend Indian Day at the Pleasant Point Indian Reservation, traditionally held the second Sunday of August. It would be my first trip back to the reservation since 1997.

Spending the day with Fred, I was impressed by the turnout and the cultural traditions on display. After a series of dances, the master of ceremonies passed around a peace pipe, which the dancers ceremoniously "smoked." At the end, the master of ceremonies took the pipe and smoked to the north, south, east and west, asking for the Creator's favor. It reminded me instantly of my own behavior and version of smoking in that Boston hotel in 1998. At the end of the day, I had no qualms or ill effects after returning to the rez.

During the first week of September, when tribal elections were held, I stayed on the reservation for a week to give Fred my moral support and work on parts of the book with him. Fred campaigned from morning until night. Unfortunately, we didn't make any headway on the project, and he lost his bid to be tribal governor by a vote of 207 to 197. He has since accepted a position with Quoddy Bay LNG, a company seeking to build a $500 million liquefied natural gas plant on parts of the reservation. The project is going very well.

On March 20, 2008, Robert "Bobbie" Newell was indicted by a federal grand jury for various crimes involving tribal misapplication of funds. The 30-count indictment cites improper criminal activity in this regard by Newell from September of 2004 to September of 2006. Newell was a tribal governor who helped fire Fred Moore from his job as police chief in July of 1992.

I have made my peace with Our Lord, and I hope to devote the rest of my private life to helping the poor, the hungry, the homeless and the ill. I'll probably work in a soup kitchen, as I've done in the past, help a few local destitute families with a little money, start a business or two that will hire impoverished minorities, that sort of thing. And I will continue to love my wife, children and grandchildren with all my heart.

EPILOGUE

St. Longinus was the Roman Centurion who pierced Christ's side with a lance during the crucifixion. He converted to Catholicism after the incident and was martyred for his belief. St. Gaspar, St. Melchoir and St. Balthasar were the three wise men who brought gifts to and visited Jesus shortly after his birth. In the year 0040, all three were baptized by St. Thomas, an apostle of Christ. Their conversion to the Catholic faith cost them their lives. They were martyred for their faith. All four died for the Greater Glory of God.

Our mutual experiences have brought Fred and I to a closer understanding of the meaning of life. During times of distress, we speak with each other often, and say prayers for one another and our families.

Over the years, Fred has steadfastly tried to help the Passamaquoddies emerge from economic depression and those efforts continue today, 16 years after the Mohawk case.

In the late spring of 2006, on a cool, clear evening, I stepped outside about 9 p.m. and gazed into the heavens. The stars and the moon were shining brilliantly. I said a prayer to Mom, Dad, Venise (my deceased sister), Father Capodanno, Vern Randolph, Schmitty and others, and beseeched Our Father to more clearly explain the meaning and purpose of life to me.

Immediately, an inner voice responded: Life is an eternal proposition. Christ's death and resurrection testifies to that. Without believing in Christ and following his teachings, all of life is essentially meaningless, crowned by an inevitable death.

However, if one believes in The Way, The Truth and The Life, life's accomplishments become truly meaningful.

Most persons on this earth believe in some sort of life after death. That is a product of tens of thousands of years of self-reflection. In my opinion, it all boils down to the barest of essentials -- good versus evil, heaven versus hell. I have tasted both. Let there be peace on earth and let it begin with me. This has been written for the Greater Glory of God.

Made in the USA
Middletown, DE
09 November 2016